Awakening the Spirit

Awakening the Spirit

The Open Wide Like a Floozy Chronicles

Cindy L. Herb

Awakening the Spirit:
The Open Wide Like a Floozy Chronicles
© 2008 by Cindy L. Herb

All rights reserved. No part of this publication may be used or reproduced in any manner whatsoever without written permission except in the case of brief quotations embodied in articles and reviews.

Manufactured in the United States of America.

For information, please contact:

The P3 Press
16200 North Dallas Parkway, Suite 170
Dallas, Texas 75248

www.thep3press.com

972-248-9500

A New Era in Publishing™

ISBN-13: 978-1-933651-37-8
ISBN-10: 1-933651-37-7
LCCN: 2008910692

Author contact information:

Cindy L. Herb

www.cherbchronicles.com

Dedication

To all my brothers and sisters who labor in humankind's continual spiritual awakening and promote the attributes of Love, Understanding, Compassion, Honesty, Honor, and Humility.

Contents

Preface ix

Acknowledgments xi

Part One

God—Our Past, Present, and Future 1

  1 What Is My Purpose? 3

Part Two

Reliving the Past 9

  2 Spirited: Supplementing What Is Lacking 11
  3 The Good News 15
  4 No Rest on Sunday 17
  5 Our Path 21
  6 Have You Seen—? 25
  7 The Force of Destruction 31
  8 Where Are You? 39
  9 A Noisy Basket 47
  10 May We Come In? 53
  11 Experience of Healing 61
  12 Exposing the Truth 65
  13 Cleanliness Is Next to Godliness 71
  14 No Hope 77
  15 Making a Deal 83
  16 The Strength of Protection 87
  17 The Stuff We Are Made Of 97
  18 Law of Attraction 103
  19 The Search for Knowledge 109

Part Three
Presenting the Discord 113
20 Imbalance of Love. 115
21 Rumblings 125
22 Damaged Love: Overlooking the Flaws 137
23 Dirty Onion Sack 143

Part Four
Changing My Future 153
24 Moving Forward. 155
25 Visiting a Shaman. 161
26 Heaven-sent 169
27 Connections. 173
28 Part of the Whole 185
29 Listening to Instincts 201
30 Mother to Mom. 209
31 Allowing God's Energy 217

About the Author

Preface

This book is intended to inspire others, and it outlines real life situations, some of which may cause the reader to view certain members of my family unfavorably. During the course of writing this book, I unexpectedly discovered that taking a path of neutrality when looking back at these circumstances has turned out to be more beneficial than I could have expected.

Acknowledgments

Charles Crooks—I am forever indebted and connected to Charles, who knew from the start that I would write a book and helped me keep my eye on the goal. I am extremely appreciative of his suggestions and many hours of careful review. Without his guidance and support, this book would not have been possible. He is not only my angel, but also a timeless, long-standing, valued friend.

Mary—Mary has always been there to listen and was the first person who encouraged me to write. More than a sister, she is one of my best friends and has provided me with a lifetime of comfort, nurturing, and love. She offered me a safe haven during the worst times of my life. She has given me so much without asking anything in return. She has my undying love, and I will forever cherish her.

Drusilla Enriquez—Endless thanks to her for sticking by me through thick and thin; she is my dearest, truest friend. I am forever grateful for our many talks. She is the best listener and has an uncanny ability to translate my convoluted gibberish, reflecting it back to me in such a way that I am able to understand it myself. From the moment I met her, I felt a strong bond, and I will always treasure her and our journey together. Thanks for all the pointers!

Angie Miller—Expressions of gratitude are due to her for the countless hours of listening to my stories and giving me valuable insight.

Sandy Marak—I value the professional pictures from Sandy at www.sandymarak.com. Special thanks to her for taking me on as a "pet" project and making me look good. Although her passion is pet photography, her talents extend far beyond.

Mark White—What would I have done without Mark's creative input during my photo shoot? Thanks for fixing my hair, helping coordinate my wardrobe, and taking the wrinkles out of my clothes.

The P3 Press, a division of Brown Books Publishing Group—My hat is off to them. From the moment we began, I felt they were the right publisher for the job. They did not disappoint and always had my best interests at heart. They are a unique group of caring, extremely helpful people. I am especially appreciative of the hand-holding from the Director of New Author Services, Cynthia Stillar-Wang. I would also like to extend kudos to editor Rachel Felts for the thorough line edit; she did not change my words, but rather made them come alive. And to all the others who contributed to the professional quality of this book . . . an enthusiastic, "Bravo!"

Part One

God: Our Past, Present, and Future

Chapter 1

What is My Purpose?

When someone is close to death and survives, it is often said, "There must be a greater purpose for you." When I was eleven years old, I almost drowned while taking a swimming test. I was tired, but I kept on swimming, eventually sinking to the bottom of the pool. The lifeguard who rescued me reiterated this very profound statement when she said, "Sweetie, thank God you are alive. He must have a greater plan for you."

There were many occasions where my life seemed to take on inherently unexpected circumstances, some of them discussed in this book. Even though I attempted to control my life, it appeared my life would take on a life of its own. It was as if, while I was aiming for a certain direction, conditions forced me in an entirely different direction. I was lacking strength. I concluded that my faith, or perception of God, was being tested.

Over time, I came to realize this turmoil was both a blessing and a veto from God. I did not know it at the time, but I was being guided to take another path. I was also being protected by some higher power. Why else would I have survived?

I imagined God had a plan for me. However, what it was, I did not know. Like most Catholic girls, or so I had supposed, I wanted to be a nun, thinking this was what God wanted. My mom constantly remarked how much I reminded her of Sister Florentine, my aunt, who was a nun. Even Sister Florentine herself made the same comments when she visited.

As I grew older, I realized I was indeed a great deal like my aunt. She and I were both very spiritual and, with each passing year, our relationship grew closer. Sister died at age eighty-four. I knew long before then, however, that I did not want to become a nun. That was definitely not my purpose.

What is my purpose? Why am I here? What is the soul? What is our real existence? What is anyone's purpose? These are fundamental questions asked throughout the ages. I, like scores of others, have asked myself these questions countless times in my life. Many people look outside themselves to find the answers, such as to others or to organized religion. I was the same.

After much contemplation, I thought I knew the answer. It was love. Yes, love! Sounds pretty solid, doesn't it? After all, just about every religion speaks to the unconditional love of God, who encompasses all, including the past, present, and future. We hear it every day. God is love. Love is all we need. Love conquers all. Love is the answer. What do you think? Is this answer valid?

Authors, poets, songwriters, and the like from every age, have all written more about love than any other emotion. Why? Do you suppose love is the most sought-after aspect of the human condition? We all have experienced some form of love in our lives, including me.

For instance, I have always felt love from my sister, Mary. I guess this is why we are so close today. I sensed it from infancy, in the very first memory I recall, when I was just twenty-one months old.

With vivid clarity, I can recount a scene when I was in the crib. My memory all takes place in the kitchen and includes orientation of doorways, furniture, and relatives. Even though I was supposedly too young to summon up the incident, my mom concurs I am correct about all the details. She cannot explain it, other than I must actually remember it.

My parents, three of my other siblings, and my mom's oldest sister and her family were eating pumpkin pie in the kitchen. Therefore, the event more than likely occurred around Thanksgiving. I do not know how I know it was pumpkin pie; I just know instinctively.

My crib was in my parents' bedroom, which was adjacent to the kitchen. It was a light chestnut-colored crib with thin, battered and scratched slats. The bedroom was quite cramped, and the crib barely fit in the room, so my mom had it parked halfway in the doorway to the kitchen.

On this particular day, everyone was crowded around a table, laughing and eating pie. Although the kitchen was very small, they seemed to be having a grand old time. I was fussing and my mom kept strolling over to my crib, stuffing a bottle in my mouth. She picked me up and then laid me back down on my back with the bottle in my mouth, hoping I would stay still and be quiet.

As soon as she walked off, I popped up, beginning to wail while looking through the jailhouse rails. I was asking for pie! She could not understand my request. What is hilarious is, as an adult, I do not even like pumpkin pie. However, at twenty-one months, I was fascinated with the goings-on in the kitchen, and I wanted some of that pumpkin pie.

One awesome thing about the whole incident was my sister Mary. She is only fourteen months older than I am, so she had to be not quite three years old at the time; yet she came up to the crib and comforted me. I still can see and hear her as she looked through those bars, saying, "What's the matter, Cindy?" She gave me love.

Although I recognized Mary's love at the time, I always associated a more impactful emotional response with the scene. It was not the emotion of love; instead, it was one of being alone and separated. I was not included in the fun that everyone else was experiencing. Furthermore, my mom reinforced this feeling whenever she tried to keep me quiet, instead of holding me in her arms, comforting and loving me, and giving me some pie.

So beginning from a very young age, I felt all alone. And because I felt isolated from the whole group, I craved love. This condition predominantly pervaded my life, starting with that first memory. I was unhappy. If my purpose in this life was love, and God loved me unconditionally, why did I not feel love? Why was I unhappy?

Even though I knew—deep in my soul—love was the answer, something was missing. Was I alone? Did I have love? Was love really the answer? These questions would plague me for almost fifty years. But God gave me clues throughout my life, and it was only a matter of time before I found the answers. Thank God I did!

When I discovered the evidence about my purpose, I changed directions. It is never too late to change directions and change your life. I am over age fifty, am not married and have no children. I used to think this was a tragedy. But wouldn't ya know it; I discovered how to be happy! We all can be happy, if we so choose.

I am happy with the choices I have made in my life. I realized that by allowing the goodness of the universe into my life, my reality and my world could and has changed. Although I am not currently married, if I so choose, I may get married in the future. Even though I do not biologically have any children, I have a chance to nurture so many more by telling my story. Humanity is my family and my children.

All the incidents that transpired in my life—whether you perceive them as good or bad—after all was said and done, guaranteed my development and devotion to spiritual work. I had to allow a new awakening to my true purpose in order to fully understand and accept the events in my life. Before I could change my reality and, therefore, alter future events, I had to realize certain happenings in my life were necessary. As I did, I also uncovered the secret to health and happiness.

That adjustment took time because I, like so many of us, was trained to think otherwise. This is the story of that new perception and the resulting spiritual awakening. It is a continued journey, available to all, allowing comprehension of true joy and purpose in life. In the process, it can inspire others with the fact that despite adversity, there is always light.

Before I could find out my purpose, I had to go back and reexamine my life and the events that emerged, awakening me to a new awareness. So to begin, let us go back to my past.

Part Two

Reliving the Past

Chapter 2

Spirited: Supplementing What Is Lacking

I was born into a family of seven children. My father was a baker, and my mother was a cake decorator. Money was very tight. Others would have considered our family poor. I learned at a very young age that if I wanted something, I had to earn it myself. That was the way it was in our family.

We came from a strict Catholic upbringing. Our mom found a way for us to receive a Catholic education, at least through the eighth grade. Later on, money was far too scarce to afford the much more expensive cost of high school, which covered freshman to senior years and was equivalent in price to college preparatory.

In grade school, we were required to wear a standard uniform, five days a week. My parents got a break on the tuition from the nuns because of our dire situation. Moreover, the fact we wore uniforms was an economic benefit for my parents. They could get along with only a couple of uniforms per kid each year. Opposed to the many outfits we would have needed, had we attended public school.

Since we did not have many clothes, my sister Mary who was not much older than I was, decided we needed to take action to alleviate our situation. She wanted to find a way to earn extra money to buy additional clothing besides the uniforms we wore to school. Most of our non-school clothes were hand-me-downs from our older sister Terry.

My older brother Tommy had his own paper route. It covered roughly three streets and ran about eight or nine city blocks long. It was located about three blocks away from our house on Bowser Avenue in Dallas. Mary and I would occasionally help him out.

He eventually stopped throwing his papers during the summer. He decided it was more lucrative to mow lawns. Although I thought it was much harder work than the paper business, he seemed to enjoy it.

It did not really bother me to wear hand-me-downs, but it seemed to disturb Mary. She was very industrious—and still is to this day—which is one of the many traits I admire about her. She made up her mind we should start our own paper route. We discussed it and then asked our parents if we could pursue our plan.

My parents did not mind, even though we were very young. It was 1966; Mary was ten, and I was nine. In fact, my dad seemed to enjoy the fact we were working and earning our own way. As for my mom, I think she thought it kept us out of trouble and out of her hair. After all, she did have seven kids. Maybe my dad had the same feelings. Anyway, with no objection from our parents, Mary and I started our own paper route.

Chapter 3

The Good News

There were two competing newspapers in the city at that time in the 1960s. One was a morning paper, the other, an afternoon/evening paper. Mary and I had a paper route that circulated *The Dallas Times Herald*, the afternoon/evening edition.

We were responsible for approximately eight city blocks, covering two streets: Lemmon and Bowser Avenues. Bowser happened to be the street on which we lived. Lemmon Avenue was one street over from us, directly behind our house. Our route had roughly 160 customers, a decent size route for those days, but smaller than the route my brother once ran.

We attempted several methods of carrying the papers before establishing a routine. We began the old-fashioned way, using a huge canvas bag provided by the local newspaper slung over the shoulder. It held many papers, which could be quite bulky depending on the day of the week. Sundays were the worst. Mary and I each lugged one of these bags. We abandoned this approach quickly, however, as the bags were too heavy for us to bear. When I recall how much they weighed us down, my back still aches.

We also had bicycles outfitted with baskets in the rear to hold the papers. There were two baskets, one on either side of the rear tire, just behind the seat. My brother Tommy, who was a whiz with tools, had engineered our bikes to accommodate the two baskets. But this too became a problem, as the papers tended to make the bike rear up in the back when filled to capacity. The amount of papers we loaded in our baskets needed careful monitoring. Often we doubled our trips back and forth, since the baskets only held a finite amount of papers. It was not very efficient.

In the end, we settled on a deserted shopping cart. It worked great! The old basket held all our papers, and we could wheel it down the street. Mary threw one side of the street, and I threw the other. We made the fastest time this way. The only drawback was the shopping cart was super noisy. It was very old and rattled loudly as we rolled it down the street or sidewalk.

Chapter 4

No Rest on Sunday

Six days a week, we threw the paper in the late afternoon. However, delivery of the Sunday edition of the paper was very early in the morning. People expected to receive their paper before the sun rose on Sunday. They read it with their morning cup of coffee.

The papers arrived on our front porch between two and three a.m. Our branch manager usually dropped them off. He had a pickup truck, filled to capacity with papers for all the rookies who worked under his supervision. It was his job to bring the papers to us, straight from the presses. Our task was to deliver them to the front door of each patron in a timely manner. Therefore, my sister and I had to go out before the sun came up to deliver the papers on time.

Mary always had an alarm clock in her head. She invariably woke, even before those papers hit the front porch. She often roused me right before they arrived and would remark, "Cindy, get up. It's time to throw the papers!"

I remember wondering how on earth she could instantly awaken, right before they delivered the papers. It was both amazing and aggravating at the same time. I never wanted to move from my spot. I had anxiety about going out alone into the dark. So she constantly urged me to get my butt out of bed every Sunday.

Once she had coaxed me out of bed, we both dressed quickly and then proceeded to the front porch to prepare the papers for delivery. Under the front-porch light we would inspect the papers, making sure he delivered the correct amount to us. If the piles we received were less than our distribution rate, we called the branch manager to tell him he shorted us. This was rare, but I do recall one such instance where this happened. My dad was up at the time and handled the call for us. We had to wait about an hour for the branch manager to fill our supply completely.

The downtown distribution center transported the newspapers to our front door in separate stacks, bound together by thick rubber bands. Each stack contained different sections of the newspaper. Each section had an alphabetical letter assigned to it.

On Sunday, there were over fifteen different sections of the paper. Most of the time, many sections of the paper were lumped together within these stacks. For instance, sections A, C, and D might be together with section B in a stack by itself. It was our job to alphabetically integrate each section into one paper prior to delivery.

Mary and I would park ourselves on the cold, stone porch between several stacks of newspapers with a box of thick rubber bands sitting between the two of us. Picking up a section here, picking up a section there, we would collate until the paper was whole. Once it was complete, we folded it in half, placed a rubber band around it, and threw it in a pile.

It was a messy job, as ink got all over our hands. It was also often rather painful, as stretching the rubber bands to the maximum often caused them to pop. Of course, our hands were in the line of fire when they snapped. This happened regularly when we assembled the massive Sunday edition, the thickest daily newspaper we delivered, with more sections and advertisements than any other day of the week.

After folding them all, one of us would clean up the loose wrapping from the delivery and put our box of rubber bands away. The other would drag out the old shopping basket that hauled all our papers out of the garage. We would then load all the papers into the rickety cart before heading out into the night. It usually took about an hour or two to complete this procedure.

Many times, my dad was up, and he would watch us assemble the papers from inside the house. Looking through the screen door, he would observe us as he sat in his favorite spot on the end of our rust-colored vinyl couch.

My dad would drink a beer and smoke a cigarette the entire time. He was often awake in the middle of the night. I think it was because his system was used to being up during the night, as he was a baker by profession.

Chapter 5

Our Path

One Sunday, on the last day of July in 1966, the papers arrived as normal. Mary, with that damn alarm-clock head of hers, jumped out of her twin bed next to mine in our bedroom, seconds before they hit the porch. I heard her familiar call, "Cindy, wake up!"

I was facing away from her, lying in my bed with my body almost touching the wall, wide-awake already—unbeknownst to her. I was listening silently in the dark for the sound of the papers as they landed on the porch. Maybe this morning they would somehow magically disappear. I was wrong. They materialized the same as they had every other Sunday.

Our room adjoined the living room, which was at the front of the house. This room was really a dining room used as a bedroom. Inside the room, there were two twin beds lining the walls opposite each other. Mary's bed was on the left, mine on the right. There was a large entryway between our dining room/makeshift bedroom and the living room. Since it was summer, our family turned on the two air conditioners at night.

However, the smaller unit in my parent's room was not in use this Sunday. Whether it was not working or my parents were attempting to conserve money, I do not know. Since it was very hot in July and the only working unit was in the living room, just about everyone in my family was sleeping in there.

This was an occasion when my dad was awake as we got up to prepare for our route. When we came into the living room, he was sitting in his usual spot on the couch, in the dark, with his legs crossed, smoking a cigarette and drinking beer. You could make out the light on the end of his cigarette as it burned. Every now and then, lit through the light of the windows coming from the street, a puff of smoke emerged from his mouth. In his hand, he was clenching his beer. Whenever he was drinking, he never seemed to put his beer down. He was always holding it. Daddy's drinking was heavier then, probably exacerbated by his recent bout of unemployment. He had not worked in weeks.

Mary and I began the process of putting together and folding the papers. We worked steadily and quietly until we finished the job.

Daddy was still awake when we switched out the porch light as we left to begin our route at around 4 a.m. that Sunday morning. Once we left, he fell fast asleep there on the couch in the living room.

My mom was always asleep at that hour. She never woke. She always slept like a freight train. More than likely, having seven children, working fulltime, handling an alcoholic husband, and worrying about money beat her down.

It usually took Mary and me approximately two hours to finish our route each Sunday morning. We had memorized the list of homes on our route, but we always kept a list with us because we had to check it as we went along, since customers were constantly added and deleted.

A new list came with the stack of papers we had received from our branch manager earlier that morning. Mary was in charge of this list.

Our home was located at 4319 Bowser Avenue, situated between Herschel Avenue and Wycliff Avenue. We wanted to effectively make a loop of our route, not wasting any time backtracking. From our house to Wycliff Avenue, there was only one apartment building and another house, as opposed to the several houses we would pass in the other direction before reaching Herschel, so we would travel southeast to Wycliff Avenue and walk one block over to Lemmon Avenue, where we would begin our route.

Chapter 6

Have You Seen—?

Back in 1966, Lemmon Avenue was not the sea of fast-food joints it is today. Instead, there were dilapidated apartment buildings, small businesses, vacant lots, and large two-story houses badly in need of paint. There were some restaurants, but not many.

The majority of our customers on Lemmon Avenue lived in apartment buildings. I remember thinking some of the apartments were ratty looking. They looked dark and foreboding. I never felt comfortable there, though I did not know why.

After reaching Lemmon, we would journey southeast towards Oak Lawn Avenue, completing that part of Lemmon Avenue. Once we reached Oak Lawn, we would walk one block back over to Bowser Avenue. From this point, we would continue the route northwest back down Bowser, towards our own home.

Bowser Avenue was primarily comprised of single-family homes. There were some apartment buildings, but these were much higher quality than those on Lemmon Avenue. For one thing, most of them had a swimming pool.

When we went collecting, I often put my foot in the pool as we passed, dreaming of swimming in it. At night, and in the darkness of the morning, each complex lit its pool so beautifully with lights. I loved the water, and it looked so good to me. I would much rather be in one of those apartment swimming pools among the shimmering lights than throwing those damn papers!

As we continued up Bowser, the first street we would come to after Oak Lawn was Reagan Street. Stepping further, we would cross Throckmorton Street, Knight Street, Douglas Avenue, Wycliff Avenue, Herschel Avenue, Prescott Avenue, and Hawthorne Avenue before we finally reached Lomo Alto, where our route ended. Once we arrived at Lomo Alto, it was simply a matter of following the natural curve of that street, to reach Lemmon Avenue once more.

On that particular Sunday Mary and I did not talk much; we worked steadily, trying to get our job done. We turned back onto Bowser, heading north. We passed Reagan Street. We passed Throckmorton Street. We passed Knight Street.

It was right past Knight, where I had to throw the apartment building resembling an old Spanish villa. I never liked tossing papers here. A guy who lived there was inclined to disturb me, whistling and trailing close behind whenever he saw me. He made me uncomfortable.

As we approached the building, that morning I hoped that he was not there. To my relief, he was not.

We passed Douglas Avenue. Soon afterward, we were passing our own house. Everyone seemed to be quiet within the home. It was dark inside. I gazed at the house as we moved past; Daddy did not appear outside to see us go by, even as the shopping cart made its rather noisy, rattling sounds. He must have fallen asleep.

We completed our block, crossed Herschel Avenue, and began throwing the next block down from where we lived. We were nearing Prescott Avenue and were almost finished with the block, and Mary had just picked up an armful of papers to throw in the apartments across the street.

From out of nowhere, a man approached as soon as Mary had disappeared.

"Have you seen a cat?" he asked.

"No," I quickly replied.

"Could you help me find my cat?"

"Well, I must finish my route, and I need to tell my sister where I'm going," I told him.

"It'll only take a few minutes. She won't even know you are gone."

I thought for a second, realizing he was probably right, and besides, my parents taught me to help others. I did not even question how his cat got loose. As far as I was concerned, he was out so early in the morning, amid the darkness, because he was looking for his cat that had run away.

I remember wondering at the time whether I had seen him before. He looked somewhat familiar. Anyway, I believed he was one of my customers, and so I followed him to assist him in locating his cat. After all, he said we would just be a minute.

When the man first came up to me, I had been standing next to our basket, grabbing some papers. I left the basket in the street, assuming Mary would stroll out any minute to continue, and I would be back, in just a second, to join her.

I walked with the man toward Prescott Avenue, where we turned right and proceeded toward Holland Avenue, which was one block over in the opposite direction from Lemmon Avenue. However, we did not go that far.

He told me to follow him into the alley between Bowser and Holland. It was twilight now, and the alley had an eerie feel to it. It was not peculiar for me to enter the alley; Mary and I often trekked through the alley on our way to the local 7-Eleven. Several houses down, we came to a dwelling that looked recognizable. *Yes*, I thought; *we threw papers to this house. I had never seen the back of the house though.*

There was a large vegetable garden growing in the yard. The vegetables came right up to a flimsy chicken-wire fence. Standing there, I wondered if this guy was the son of the lady who lived there. Whenever we went collecting, we never got a good look at him. Still, I was not sure.

"My cat's in the vegetable garden. I saw him over there. Can you crawl under the fence and get him?" He pointed to a section of the garden where some plants were growing close to the house. As he spoke, he fidgeted with the bottom of the fence, as if trying to make room for me to crawl under it. "Here kitty, kitty," he called.

As I drew closer, he suddenly changed his mind and said, "Oh no, he's not here. I think he ran down the alley." I was somewhat relieved, because I thought I would cut myself as I wiggled under the narrow, sharp fence. I had nothing to protect my legs or arms. I was wearing a white, short-sleeved, cotton blouse that buttoned in the front, a pair of old, faded red shorts, and a pair of worn tennis shoes.

He now looked back in the direction from which we had just traveled. He stood and started moving back towards Prescott, coaxing me to follow. He was out in front of me, but he periodically looked over his shoulder to make sure I was following him. He crossed Prescott and advanced into the alley on the other side of the street, moving towards Hawthorne Avenue.

It was at this point that I became hesitant. "I think my sister's going to get mad at me. I better get back," I said as we trekked along.

"Oh, I saw him run right up here, and I know we can find him quickly," he said as he pointed straight ahead. He seemed to hoof it much faster now. As he paced along, I fell behind, vacillating about whether to abandon the search. We crossed Hawthorne Avenue.

All I could think about was getting back to Mary. We had been gone more than a few moments. *How long could this take?* As I caught up to him, he was stirring around some Pampas grass in someone's backyard. Pampas grass is a tall grass that grows in large clumps and bears huge feathery white plumes in the summertime. It can reach several feet high, and this clump was taller than this man's height. I figured the cat must be there.

I floundered, moving closer to him. He was kneeling down by the big bushy grass. He was looking at something under the tall blades. There were also clusters of red

Cannas all around the yard. Cannas have wide leaves that resemble banana leaves. They can grow several feet tall and support a rather hefty flower at the top of their stalk. Whoever owned this yard had a love for high grasses and big flowers. It was impeccably groomed, and it looked good. But after that day, I would hate Pampas grass, Cannas, and the color red for a very long time.

Chapter 7

The Force of Destruction

I advanced nearer to him, observing his interest in the immense grass. He had spread some of the leaves and was peering into the thick mass. It was then that he gazed at me and motioned me to come even closer. He asked, "Can you reach in there and get my cat?"

Without hesitation, I obeyed him, bent down on all fours, and began reaching under the grass. He was kneeling beside me on my left. I did not like looking under this grass. I asked myself, "What if something else is under there, like a snake?"

Suddenly, without warning, the man grabbed me! To muffle my screams, he covered my mouth with his hand. I kicked in his arms, trying to break his hold as he was taking me down. However, it was to no avail. He was too big and overpowering. I could hear my whimpers through the weight of his hand on my mouth. Within seconds he had thrown me down on my back, pinning me to the ground.

Seconds later, he got me under control and then managed to drag me about a foot away from the substantial Pampas grass. As soon as he moved me, he flung himself on top of me. Situated there, between two clumps of Pampas grass, we came to rest. There was another clump just above my head. We were out of sight of both the owner's house and the street. It was the perfect cover for his deed.

Before I knew it, he was quickly pulling off my red shorts and panties. He ripped open my white, cotton top—ripping the buttons off in the process—exposing my flat prepubescent breasts. He tossed my shorts and panties, with swift force, several feet from where I lay. As he did so, he knocked off one of my tennis shoes. He grabbed it and wildly threw it somewhere off in the distance.

I was now lying almost fully naked on the lawn, except for one shoe and my torn blouse—completely exposed in such a way that had never happened in my entire life. I was just nine years and five months old. I was in a state of panic. I felt myself go numb, as if I left my body.

It all happened so rapidly, my mind could not even comprehend it until years later. I was shaking all over as he methodically spread my two young legs, opening them very wide.

"Close your eyes and don't look at me! I will hurt you if you look at me! Put your hands over your eyes and cover them. Do you understand?"

"Uh-huh."

I answered, but the words seemed to hang in my throat. I did not want to see. I closed my eyes tight and, as instructed, put my hands over them. I was shedding tears quietly.

Then, horrifically, I felt something thrust inside of me. It hurt! It burned! *Please stop*! It was constant, over and over, in and out. I wanted to scream, but I held my screams within, heeding his warning. I was shaking with fear. Secretly I was shouting, "Get off of me!" He smelled of sweat and cigarettes. It was the most despicable and disgusting feeling. It seemed to go on forever, though in reality it only lasted a short while.

Meanwhile, Mary had come out of the apartment building to find the deserted shopping basket. She assumed I was throwing papers somewhere up the street, just out of sight. Thinking I would stroll out from someone's doorway any minute, she rolled the cart a little further along.

She crossed Prescott Avenue, picked up some papers, and threw nearly half the block before she realized I was nowhere in sight. She glimpsed back down the street but did not see me. At this moment, she became alarmed. Mary crossed over to the other side of Bowser, checking houses to determine whether I had thrown any papers to our assigned customers. She decided to backtrack on my side of the street to try to locate me. As she retraced her steps, she checked each house where I should have thrown a paper.

She was nearly a full block down, when she discovered where I had last thrown a paper. She was much further along on her side of the block. Panicked, as we had always stayed together in the past, she frantically called out to me.

"Cindy, Cindy, where are you?"

I did not answer.

The man pulled out of me and lifted off me, but he still had my body pinned between his legs. I continued crying, quietly, so as not to make him mad. I still had my eyes clenched closed and covered with my hands. I waited, hoping he was letting me go free. But I was wrong.

He asked, "Do you know what a Peter is?" He was sitting on me now, instead of laying on me. I had no idea about what he was referring.

"No."

"Do you know the thing that hangs between your dad's legs? Maybe you have brothers who have them also. That is a Peter."

Oh my God! I had never imagined what my dad had between his legs. I had seen him in his boxer shorts, but frankly, I was not interested in what was between his legs. This guy put it square in my mind's eye. It was not a pretty scene. *Is that what he just inserted inside me? Wait a minute. Is he talking about the thing a man uses when he goes to the bathroom?* He said my brothers had them. That was gross! It was at that moment that he progressed on to the most depraved act.

"I want you to put my Peter in your mouth and suck on it."

I wanted to scream out, *Put that nasty thing in my mouth! Are you kidding? It has been in your pants and you pee with it! You just stuck it in my own body, where my urine is!* I thought I was going to vomit.

Apparently, he was not satisfied and decided he needed more. Before I could process what he had just requested, he followed his words again with the warning, "Don't forget to keep those eyes closed. I wouldn't want to hurt you," as if he had not already hurt me.

"Take your hands off your eyes, but don't open them. Now take my Peter, hold it, and put it in your mouth. OK?"

What! He wanted me to actually touch and hold that thing! Oh my God! I was going to die. I could not utter a word; acknowledgement stuck in my throat.

He shifted his lower body to my face and slowly pried each one of my hands off my eyes, placing them on his penis. I was seriously trembling, too afraid to look up to grab his penis myself. I touched it. It was rock hard and rather large.

"OK, put it in your mouth and suck."

I slowly forced his "Peter" into my mouth. As he came down on me, his smell grew more intense—cigarettes, sweat, and what I imagined was urine. It was all I could do to keep from heaving right there on the spot. The Peter in my mouth was extremely rank. It was huge and totally filled my mouth.

Although I was supposed to keep my eyes shut, I opened them momentarily, catching a glimpse of something—body parts. I was not sure what. I felt as if I was choking. Something foul and warm suddenly exploded in my mouth, and then I did begin choking. I never sucked it. I could not. I thought he just urinated in my mouth.

He finally pulled out. It was over. I was coughing and heaving. His bodily fluids spilled out of my mouth, onto my face and neck, along with the contents of my stomach. I turned my head to deposit the vile contents onto the lawn. I could not get rid of the fluids fast enough.

Before I knew it, he was finally getting off me. I was still throwing up and coughing. It was then I started sobbing. The taste would not leave my mouth. It was a polluted taste that would haunt me for the rest of my life. I would never be able to kiss any man who smoked. With my eyes still shut, and through my sobbing, I could hear him zipping up his pants.

"Be quiet!" He was upset. "Don't tell anyone about this, or I'll get you again—and your sister! Keep those eyes closed and do not move until you count to fifty. Count out loud, so I can hear you. OK? Then you can get up, get dressed, and go home. But make sure you do not tell your parents about this, or I'll get you again! Start counting now." He sounded menacing that time.

At last, he left me there in the yard—exposed, counting, and crying. "One, two, three, four, five, six . . ."

After several minutes of searching up and down the street, calling my name and receiving no answer, Mary decided to finish the route and then go inform my parents. She did not really know what else to do. The route had to be finished, and we were on the last leg of it anyway. All the while, she was unnerved. She worked fast, first taking papers to each house that I had left without a paper. She then continued the route, uneasy and alone.

I counted to fifty, and as I was doing so, my weeping became more intense. Instinctively, I had put my hands back over my eyes as soon as he ordered me to be quiet. His warning had frightened me further, as if that were possible. I was laying flat on my back, almost utterly naked, and counting. But the only thought going through my mind at that moment was the all-encompassing terror for Mary. *Was he out there now, looking for her? Oh my God! Help her! Save her!* I had to get dressed as fast as I could to warn her. I counted as quickly as possible, so I could leave. I had at last reached the end, " . . . forty-seven, forty-eight, forty-nine, fifty!"

Jumping up, I began the search for my clothes, all the while crying. To my surprise, they were not resting right next to me. By a large cluster of Pampas grass to my left, I found my red shorts and underwear. My panties were halfway inside my shorts. My absent tennis shoe seemed to have disappeared. I had to look hard for it and was close to abandoning the search, when I noticed it wedged in the bottom leaves of the Pampas grass he had been inspecting when the whole incident began.

I quickly started to put on my clothes. My shorts and panties were much like a lid from a sardine can, peeled back with a key. I had to unroll them in order to dress again. I was bawling by that point and shaking so hard that it was difficult to stand and dress. I felt faint, and nearly fell over as I slipped on my tennis shoe without even bothering to untie it.

For a moment, I was so disoriented I did not even realize that I was already wearing my blouse, and I began to search for it. All I could see was my exposed chest. It finally dawned on me that I was wearing the shredded piece of fabric, with the buttons torn off. I had no other choice but to hold the front closed with my hands.

Mary had drudged her way to the end of our route on Bowser Avenue. Lomo Alto curves, running into Lemmon Avenue. Tom Thumb Grocery Store was on Lomo Alto in a little shopping strip. Down from there was a drugstore, on the corner of Lomo Alto and Lemmon Avenue.

There was an old, yellowish-brown, brick apartment building on our route directly behind the Tom Thumb. Whenever we finished throwing papers on Bowser Avenue, we would cut through the alley behind this apartment building, emerging in the parking lot of the drugstore. This was the speediest way for us to continue our route on Lemmon Avenue, without walking all the way around via Lomo Alto.

As I surfaced from Hawthorne Avenue, Mary was in the yellowish-brown apartment building, delivering the last of the Bowser Avenue papers. She had our shopping basket with her at the back of the building, where she was preparing to exit into the alley.

Chapter 8

Where Are You?

As I staggered back out onto Hawthorne Street, the sun was just starting to rise. Before I moved any further, I surveyed the area to see if my attacker was anywhere in sight. I concluded he was gone and took off running in the direction of Bowser. When I arrived at the corner of Bowser and Hawthorne, I started up the street towards Lomo Alto in pursuit of Mary and our shopping cart.

"Mary, are you there? Help! I need you! Mary, where are you?" There was no answer, and, even worse, there was no shopping cart.

In a split second, my mind went wild. *Oh no! He has her!*

I was not even thinking rationally. The shopping cart would probably be abandoned in plain view had the man enticed her away. Instead of thinking of this option, I lost control of my faculties. I immediately raced in the direction of Lemmon Avenue, in the hopes that I would stumble onto Mary. Maybe he did not get her. I prayed, *PLEASE, GOD, SAVE MY SISTER FROM THAT MAN!*

As I reached Lemmon Avenue, I saw that she was not in sight. I knew that if that man had not taken her, she surely would have made it to this point already. After all, the sun was almost completely up. I was all alone, standing on the corner of Hawthorne and Lemmon Avenues, bawling and screaming her name at the top of my lungs.

I turned and headed in the direction of our house, thinking I needed to get back home; it was only a couple of blocks away. Running down the middle of Lemmon Avenue, screaming for Mary, I held my blouse tight about my chest, sobbing buckets. I was completely unaware of my surroundings. With every step I took, I became more hysterical.

"Mary! Mary! Oh my God, where are you? Help! Help me, somebody!"

Unexpectedly, a police cruiser pulled up beside me and abruptly stopped. As the policeman rolled down his window, I immediately froze on the spot. I was unaware of the few passing cars, slowing to gawk.

"What's going on here? Are you OK? Why are you out here by yourself?"

As the policeman talked, he had both hands locked firmly on the steering wheel, as if he were going to choke it. He was forceful with his questions, making me even more distressed.

Like any other child of the '60s, I had a healthy fear of the law. This was, in part, due to the non-constructive publicity of the Dallas police department after the Kennedy assassination. That fiasco occurred when I was just six years old. The media blasted the news all over print, radio, and television. Since there were no parental controls in our family, naturally, I was exposed to an enormous amount of negative media, and the events of that day had a lasting effect on me.

Despite my fear of the man in the cruiser, I needed help. "A man! A man got me and now he is going to get my sister! Help! Help me!" I was shaking so ferociously, the policeman instantly reached out, lightly touching my hand.

"There, there, calm down. What is your name?" he asked. His demeanor had changed. He somehow softened. I instantly felt less agitated.

"Cindy," I sobbed.

As he was stroking my hand through the window, I noticed another officer sitting next to him. The officer in the passenger's seat picked up a microphone in the police car. I could hear a bunch of crackling coming from the radio.

"What are you doing out here, honey?" he asked again.

"I was throwing my paper route with my sister, but a man asked me to help him find his cat. And, oh my God, he got me!" My crying intensified for a moment. "Now he is going to try and get my sister. I have to warn her!"

As he was listening to me, the other officer pressed a button on the microphone, paused briefly, and then chatted back and forth with an unknown voice on the other end.

He was apparently giving a report back to a dispatcher. I could not understand everything he was saying, but soon he completed his conversation and focused all his attention back on me.

The officer on the driver's side slowly opened his door and stepped out of the car. He had a little brown book with him, where the pages flipped over. He began writing furiously, and after several moments, he asked, "Cindy what?"

I knew they were going to help me—my breathing slowed and I became less anxious. Still, I was worried about Mary. "You have to find my sister! That man is going to get her!"

Needing to settle me down, the policeman decided to put me in his squad car. Gingerly, he caressed my shoulders, guiding me to the passenger side of the car. He opened the door and motioned for the other officer to retreat to the backseat. He then requested I sit inside, on the front seat. As I slid in, he walked around to enter on the other side. But another cruiser pulled up just as he was about to open his door.

The other patrol-car driver rolled down his window, and the two men conversed for several minutes. The policeman in the backseat climbed out of our car to join the conversation. In the meantime, I sat in the car, alone with my thoughts. I was crying, sighing, and worrying about Mary, wondering if life would ever be the same.

I glanced up upon hearing the driver's door and backseat door opening. It was the policemen returning to the vehicle. The vinyl seat crackled as the driver slipped behind the wheel. He grabbed the microphone and started uttering in code. I caught the phrase " . . . I'm taking her to Parkland Hospital."

He placed the car in gear, put his foot on the gas, and, before I had a chance to respond, headed in the opposite direction of our house.

"Honey, I'm taking you to the hospital. A doctor must examine you. Do not worry. The other patrol car is going to find your sister, then explain to your parents what has happened. Your mother will meet us at the hospital."

Whisked off, I felt no reaction as he continued speaking. I did not hear anything after "your mother will meet us at the hospital." If ever I needed my mom, now was the time. I was relieved to hear she was coming to the hospital.

As we were driving down Lemmon Avenue, I saw Mary roaming with the basket near the corner of Prescott and Lemmon. I started shouting, interrupting his words. "There's Mary. Oh thank God!"

He immediately slowed the car. At the same time, he grabbed the mike from the dash between us and began chattering into it. I was oblivious to his conversation. As we approached her, I rolled down my window. Mary was looking baffled.

Exasperated, she briskly marched closer and yelled, "Cindy, where have you been? I have been looking all over for you!"

As she was speaking, a police car whizzed past us on the right, jumping across the median of the street. It then screeched to a halt in front of Mary and her basket, startling her and stopping her dead in her tracks. Our car caught up to both the other patrol car and Mary and came to a stop. The officer next to me rolled down his window to converse with another patrolman in the other car. One of the officers in the other cruiser stepped out and signaled Mary to come over. She complied.

As I did not have the best vantage point, sitting across from the action, I could only faintly hear him ask her, "Is your name Mary?"

I saw her nod yes. All the while, she was trying to peer into my patrol car to see me. I am sure she was wondering what the heck happened. I was comforted, somewhat, knowing Mary was all right. The man could not have gotten her too, or she would have been a mess. Thank God.

The other patrolman appeared at our car, leaning his head through the driver's side window. He glanced over in my direction, inspecting my appearance. I was still clutching my blouse. I put my head down, suddenly very conscious of my appearance and feeling ashamed. I could hear him tell the officer sitting next to me, "It's her sister. I will try to get the rest of the information out of her. Go ahead and take her on to Parkland."

Parkland Hospital is a community hospital in Dallas, Texas. It was in this emergency room in 1963 where President John F. Kennedy expired. The hospital is located just a few blocks south of Inwood Road on Harry Hines Boulevard. It was about a seven- to ten-minute drive from our house to the hospital, depending on traffic. It took us less than five minutes to arrive there that Sunday.

Before I could even talk to Mary, we were speeding away from her. The officer's foot pressed so hard on the gas, I could feel my heart jump to the back of my chest. The houses and businesses on Lemmon Avenue quickly flashed by my window. Sitting there in the squad car, listening to the occasional squawk of the radio, I began to sense that I was dirty. I still had the taste of that man in my mouth. I wondered if these policemen could smell me. *God, I hope not! They probably think I am filthy too*! Instinctively, I pulled my blouse even tighter.

"Did you know the man?"

The officer's voice sounded dreamlike. I was in shock. For the next several hours, I responded to every question in a trancelike state. I answered, but from where the answers came, only God knew.

"I don't know." I did not know either. I was not sure of anything. I initially thought he was perhaps a customer, but somehow I neglected to tell this to the officer.

"What did he look like?"

"I don't know. He told me to keep my eyes closed and I did. I did not want to see. It was horrible!"

I had calmed down, but with the officer's questioning, the tears began flowing freely once more.

"Where were your parents? Don't they go out with you when you throw papers?"

I never liked going out alone on Sunday morning, but I never thought it was wrong of my parents to let us go by ourselves. I figured they would not let us do anything that could possibly harm us. They had to love us enough to protect us. Now it seemed this officer was questioning their judgment.

I sheepishly answered, "No, they are home asleep." I was relieved to see we were stopping, which meant the probing questions would stop.

Chapter 9

A Noisy Basket

Mary was stunned when she discovered from the police that some man had taken me. She did not really understand what that meant. She only knew there was trouble. From what she could see of me sitting in the car, I looked bad. They did not let her speak to me, and she was just as nervous as I was about talking to the police and wanted to cooperate.

The policemen asked her a series of questions. They wanted to know our full names and address, a description of the area we generally threw papers, where she lost track of me, and what time we had left the house. In addition, they asked her whether she had seen me go off with the man and if we had seen any suspicious men around. They also inquired the whereabouts of my parents and the reason we were unescorted. She answered all their questions as best she could, and they wrote everything in a little book.

It turned out that the old shopping cart that made our deliveries so much more efficient may have alerted the perpetrator—as the police referred to him—to our position. They surmised he knew when we would arrive, based on the noise factor of the basket as it rattled along. The man was waiting patiently for us that Sunday morning, like a cunning cat. According to the police, he had probably been watching us for some time and had seen we were unaccompanied. He had perfect opportunity and he took it. They would keep an eye out for him because he was a predator and might try again. The police revealed all the information they discovered to my parents later.

In the meantime, the ragged basket that had turned out to be bad luck for us on that particular morning was also becoming a thorn in the side for the police squad car. Satisfied with her answers for the time being, the police wanted to take Mary on a tour of the neighborhood to establish the exact spot where she last saw me. However, they were having some problems getting the cart in the police car. The basket was too bulky to fit in either the trunk or the back seat.

"I only live about a block down and a block over. I'll just walk home with my basket," Mary told the police.

"Oh no, young lady, you are not going anywhere by yourself. This other officer can take your basket, by foot, to your home. We will meet him back at your house. While he is doing that, I want you to get in my car and take a ride with me. I will take you home to your parents as soon as we visit the area you last saw Cindy."

The two officers spoke for a few minutes, and then he ushered her into the car, leaving the other officer standing with the basket in the street. The sun had completely risen, bringing on another hot summer day. The low that morning was eighty-one degrees, and by the day's end, the temperature would be elevated to a high of one hundred and one.

He slowly pulled away from the median and asked her for directions, whereby she pointed to Herschel Avenue. He aimed the car on that course and they inched slowly down the street. While on this bearing, he focused on every house, bush, driveway, car, van, etc. He was looking for any suspicious characters. Mary directed him to drive down Bowser Avenue and showed him the location, just before Prescott, where she had last seen me. They continued meandering through the neighborhood, block after block, until the policeman was satisfied the perpetrator was no longer around.

Mary had never been in a police car before. It was both scary and exciting. She, just like me, received the opportunity to ride in the front seat. There was a big, black radio in the front of the car. It was between the dash and the floor of the car, situated in the middle of the seat between the driver's side and the passenger's side of the automobile. Attached to it was a long, black, spiral cord. At the end of the cord, a thick, square microphone protruded, with a button at the top of it. There were several knobs and dials on the radio.

As they drove along, Mary could hear voices coming across the radio; one moment she heard a few words, then abruptly there would be silence. Periodically, the police officer picked up the mike, pressed the button, and spoke into it. It was all new and fascinating for a ten-year-old girl. Finally he pulled up in front of our house at 4319 Bowser, and the ride was over. Waiting on the sidewalk with the empty shopping basket, was the other officer. Before she knew it, he was opening her door.

Inside our home, everyone else was sound asleep, having no idea of the drama going on outside. My dad never made it to his own bed. He had fallen fast asleep on the long living room couch. My baby sister Patty, who was age four, shared the couch with him, tucked into a fetal position on the end.

Both she and my other little sister Jeanne, who was five, did not really have a bedroom. Instead, my parents kind of put them wherever they could find the space. That morning, Patty was on the couch and Jeanne was sleeping in a matching, rust-colored, vinyl overstuffed chair.

My two brothers—Tommy, who was twelve, and Paul, who was six—had their own bedroom next to my parents' bedroom. However, they had wandered into the living room during the night, as was often the case during the hot summer, to find comfort from the cool mist of the air conditioning unit. Both of them were camped out on the wooden floor.

My oldest sister, Terry, who was fourteen, had her own bedroom at the front of the house. She could benefit from the air conditioner just by opening her bedroom door, allowing the air to flow into her room, so she was in the comfort of her own bed when the police officers guided Mary by the hand to the front porch. As Mary was about to dash inside the door, one of them instinctively pulled her back.

Chapter 10

May We Come In?

It was about seven a.m. when there was a pounding knock on the door at 4319 Bowser Avenue. My dad, who was sleeping on the couch, swiftly sat up just as my mom came bolting into the room from their back bedroom.

"Who on earth could that be?" she asked, sounding worried.

The noise had startled Tommy, who was usually up early. In a flash, he was at the window peering out, like a turtle sticking its head out of its shell.

"It's the police!" he said. His adrenaline was rushing. *Who is in trouble?* he wondered.

"Shut up and get away from that window!" Daddy quickly snapped as he slipped on some trousers. My mom ran to find a housecoat. Terry, who had been slumbering in her bed, heard the commotion and came to stand, with her arms crossed over her chest, in her doorway by the living room, intently watching the scene unfolding. Paul also awakened, sitting up on the floor amid his covers and blankets, still half snoozing. Jeanne was dead to the world in the armchair. Patty, on the end of the couch, stirred from the movement of Daddy but remarkably remained fast asleep. Tommy, who had shot over to the window, skedaddled back to his spot on the floor. He wanted to be front and center for this.

As Daddy opened the door, my mom rushed into the room, fastening a robe around her waist.

"Mr. Herb?" The policeman sounded official.

"Yes?" said my dad, as he opened the door wider.

"May we come in?"

It was at that second, that he and my mom noticed Mary standing stoically on the front porch.

"What has happened? Where is Cindy?" My mom sounded alarmed.

"We need talk to you, Mr. Herb. There has been an incident. May we come in?" The policeman's voice was direct and to the point.

Daddy robotically swung the door wide open, as my mom gave her standard line in any crisis, "Oh my God!" She stood there, frozen in a stunned state, as Daddy waved both policemen into the room. My mom could not even muster enough stamina to hug Mary, who was also a victim in all this unpleasantness. One of the officers led Mary into the house, and when my mom did not move towards her daughter, he planted her on the sofa. My mom appeared to be in her own world.

The policemen took inventory of the surroundings and were somewhat shocked to see the living conditions. They noticed several beer cans on the coffee table, along with numerous cigarette butts in the ashtray. It was obvious that there were quite a few people in this family sleeping in the front room instead of the bedrooms. The two youngest were sound asleep, and another one—a boy slightly older—was sitting groggily on the floor, surrounded by a sheet and a thin blanket. It appeared that the teenage son also spent the night on the floor, since his covers were still evident. The officers noticed yet another child, a teenage daughter, standing in a doorway connected to the living area. They were trying to speculate how many children these people actually had.

Daddy interrupted their thoughts. "Officer, is Cindy in trouble? What did she do?"

It was typical for my dad to assume one of his kids would have misbehaved.

One of the officers responded, "No, sir. Could I speak with you and your wife alone?" As he spoke, he extended one arm, gesturing for them to head into the room Mary and I shared.

My dad looked puzzled but said, "Sure."

However, before my dad left the room, he gave a strict warning to the remaining six kiddoes there, "You kids stay here!"

With that stern statement, Daddy and Mom stepped out of the room with the officer following them, marching clear into the breakfast nook to talk. Before the officer left the room, he turned around to the other officer and motioned for him to stay behind. He wanted his partner to stand guard at the door so my brothers and sisters could not hear what our parents were discussing with the police.

It was intimidating to the young people in the household, seeing this man in a dark, navy blue uniform, standing with his hands folded across his chest. Like a formidable sentry, the officer had a gun on one hip and a bully stick on the other. They did not dare cross that doorway. However, no matter how vigilant the police were at protecting my brothers and sisters from the ugly truth, it was in vain. Everyone could hear my dad's outrage through the walls, and Terry and Tommy, being older, understood.

"We are pretty sure your daughter has been raped."

"What! Who did that to her? I'll kill that son of a bitch! Where is he? God damn it, I'll kill him!"

Clenching his fists, my dad started to race out of the house, thinking the man was in the squad car. Before he could budge a foot, the officer restrained him.

"Sir, please. Calm down." His voice was composed and unruffled. "The perpetrator has not been apprehended as yet. Your daughter has not been able to identify him. Frankly, we are not sure she will be able to. She appears to be in a state of shock."

Finally my mom spoke, "What about Mary, did he get her too?"

"No, ma'am. She apparently did not witness the crime. She was throwing her papers in some apartments when your other daughter was abducted."

"Oh, thank God!" Mom exclaimed.

"Where did this happen?" Daddy interrupted.

"Just down the street, sir. We are not exactly sure where the actual rape occurred. We only know where he abducted her. We have not been able to take your daughter through the neighborhood to locate the crime scene, because we thought it wise to get her to a hospital first. She is in such a poor state, she probably could not tell us where it happened anyway."

"What do you mean?" my mom asked.

"As I said earlier, she is in a state of shock. When our patrol car found her, she was running down the middle of Lemmon Avenue in a hysterical fit, screaming at the top of her lungs. She did not seem to know where she was. She was in danger of being hit by a car."

"I want that son of a bitch found and prosecuted, God damn it! Do you hear me?" My dad could not get over his anger.

"Will there be a trial?" Mom suddenly inquired.

"If we find the perpetrator, it is up to the prosecutor to decide. If so, your daughter might need to testify against him to put him in jail. But do not worry about that right now. First, I need you to come . . . "

Daddy does not even let him finish speaking, "There's going to be a trial, God damn it! If you find this guy, I want him to fry!"

"Yes sir."

The officer looked over at my mom. "Like I was saying, I want you to come with me to Parkland Hospital. We have taken Cindy there, and a doctor will examine her. We told her we would bring her mother to the hospital. She is expecting to see you. Can you get dressed and come with me?"

"Yes, I'll go. Just give me a minute."

With that, my mom went to her bedroom and changed quickly.

It took only five minutes for her to dress; she threw on a dress and some nylons, pulled on her pumps, brushed her hair, put on some lipstick, and grabbed her purse. Mom came out of the back bedroom to find her youngsters pelting the two police officers with questions. Tommy, especially, was interested in the guns they had on their belts.

"Can I hold that gun?" he asked.

"No, son. This is too dangerous for you."

It appeared that my dad had vanished. As my mom exited the house with the policemen, she found him on the front porch with his arms crossed, smoking his cigarette. He stared off blankly into the distance.

Before she left, she told the rest of the children, who were now all sitting in the front living room, "You kids be good while I'm gone. Do not upset your Daddy. I'll be back soon. Terry, I want you to help take care of the little ones. OK?"

Perhaps it was because my dad was so very loud and cussed within earshot of youngsters in the next room, but the policemen did not question my parents about why they allowed us to go out on our own in the first place. However, as soon as they had my mom alone in the police car, they asked, "Ma'am, can you tell us why Mary and Cindy were out throwing papers by themselves so early in the morning?"

My mom's defenses shot up quickly. "Those two little boogers, they always left the house on their own, without waking us. I work hard and sleep soundly. I did not hear them go out. We had told them before to get us up, but they never did. I never thought anything like this could happen."

The officer seemed satisfied, and did not ask any more questions.

My mom's mind was racing, however. The thought of a man raping her child brought forward ugly memories from her past. She fought to hold back her tears. She would not permit herself to shed a single drop. Her paternal grandfather had always fondled her whenever he got the chance. As far as my mom knew, he also "messed with" one of her two older sisters, but that sister was ornery and much braver than my mom had been. The sister was better at fending him off and, later, became a Catholic nun at age fifteen, remaining in the convent until she died at age eighty-four.

My mom had never told anyone about her encounters as a small child with her paternal grandfather, not even her parents or her husband. When shown pictures of him, she just commented, "I never liked going to his house."

I found out the ugly truth when, as an adult, I confronted her about my rape and her lack of parental protection. She broke down, confiding in me that she, too, had experience with inappropriate sexual behavior. My mother relayed the story of her grandfather and his escapades. She said she was only about five or six when the first incident with him happened. I asked her why she did not tell her parents. Her answer: "I was too ashamed." Her thinking directly influenced the rest of her actions on the day of my rape.

Chapter 11

Experience of Healing

Experiences in my formative years had made me leery of medical staff. As we pulled to a halt in front of an entryway marked "Emergency," although I was still in a state of shock, additional images quickly began racing through my mind. These images were of past dealings with doctors, nurses, and hospitals. The first encounter I had with a hospital was at age five.

My mom had just given birth to my youngest sister, Patty, at Parkland Hospital. My mom hemorrhaged about two months before Patty was born. At that age, I did not understand where babies came from. I only knew that my mom was going to have a baby. She started bleeding in the middle of the night, resulting in my dad rushing her to the emergency room. When we awoke the next morning, we found the bloody towels left on the bathroom floor. It was quite traumatic for my young mind. I had never seen so much blood. I thought the baby, had just popped out of my mom's stomach.

About a week later, my mom returned home. She was still pregnant, with her belly bulging. In a few months, she went back to the hospital, delivering Patty on July 23, 1962. However, when she came home, it was obvious she was not a hundred-percent. She walked slowly and looked tired. I had missed her terribly when she was gone, and I wanted to jump in her lap, but I was not allowed to because of her obvious pain. I thought the hospital had done this to her.

More images shot through my head as the policeman opened the door for me, motioning me to exit the vehicle. Because my mom had Patty at Parkland, a community hospital, she was eligible for special nursing services and community aid based on economic need. Therefore, shortly after Patty was born, a nurse began coming to the house. She had red hair and green eyes, dressed completely in white, wore white shoes, carried a black bag, and had a million red freckles on her, even on her face. This nurse administered many of our required childhood shots. I never liked those shots. They hurt!

As we walked into the same hospital on that fateful Sunday morning of July 31, 1966, I became more and more anxious. Perhaps, the doctors were going to give me another shot! I had already been through enough today.

I did not know if I could handle a shot. I was praying my mom would arrive soon. She would understand how much I hated shots.

The worst needle incident, I began to recall, involving that red-haired, skinny nurse, happened at the clinic inside Parkland Hospital. The clinic had a huge waiting room, accommodating well over a hundred patients. Filled to capacity, the room contained many people sitting around waiting to see the doctor or nurse. We had been sitting for several hours, waiting to see someone. I knew I was going to get a shot that day, and the anticipation of the pain was making the waiting even worse for me.

When they called us, my mom had to drag me down the hall, kicking and screaming. She left my siblings in the waiting room, with my oldest sister Terry to look after them. I am sure that my mom was embarrassed to death by my behavior. After pulling me into the doctor's office, there was the freckled nurse, waiting patiently. She told my mom to pull down my underpanties. I realized she was going to give me a shot in my butt!

My mom, as instructed, sat down on a chair, pulling me across her lap. I was screaming and hollering. Overpowered by the smell of alcohol, the nurse swabbed my bottom, as part of the sterilization process in preparation for the shot. There was a picture of Jesus's Last Supper on the wall. The only thing my mom could think to say as freckle face was stabbing me was, "Look at the pretty picture."

At the time, I thought, "Forget that picture, and get that needle out of me! It hurts like heck!"

I jerked back into consciousness as the officer led me into a crowded and noisy emergency room. It reminded me of the crowded clinic where I used to get shots. I began to panic.

Chapter 12

Exposing the Truth

As he sat me in an empty chair, I was cognizant of others gaping at me. Possibly, my disheveled appearance, with a torn and dirty blouse, fed the flame of interest, causing others to send their attention towards me. Their eyes cut into me deeply. I did not like it. Before I sat down, I was overly apprehensive about seeing the doctor. Now, I wanted to get out of this room any way I could.

I suppose it was because I had a police escort, but I did not have to remain in the crammed room for long. Within minutes, a woman came up to us and began to lead me down a crowded hall. It was good to be quickly ushered away from those piercing eyes. I imagined they wanted to know the gory details.

The woman escorted me to a smaller room, where there were a couple of tables used to examine patients. The staff could pull a thin curtain between each of the tables, thus deeming the area private. However, it was far from private. You could hear every detail of what was going on, just one curtain over.

The woman instructed me to get up on the table. I did so, curling up into the fetal position. The table was metal with a thin covering of cushiony vinyl. It was extremely uncomfortable. I was cold, so the woman gave me a blanket before exiting the room. It felt wonderful to cover my body completely. I felt hidden from the outside world. I waited on top of the table for what seemed like an eternity.

I did not really understand why the policeman had brought me to the hospital. I just wanted to go home. I was scared and confused. The next thing I knew, a female nurse pranced into the tiny room, handed me a sheet, pulled the curtain shut, and then instructed me to take off my clothes.

"What? Why do I have to do that?" I yelped.

"Don't worry, sweetie. The doctor is coming down to examine you. He needs to check you out to make sure you are OK." She tried to be reassuring, but I was not buying it.

"No. I don't want to take off my clothes."

As she was talking, she began transforming the table before my eyes. At the foot of the table, she pulled out two metal arms. These extended out and up, like a set of arms stretched out before you, but bent at the elbow.

"Ok, honey. Start taking off your clothes. Your mommy will be here any minute."

I did not budge, emphatically responding, "No!"

The nurse looked perturbed. She paused and then walked out of the room.

I thought, "I'm saved."

About five minutes later, the nurse returned accompanied by my mom and a male doctor. Seeing my mom, I felt great relief and start crying immediately. My mom responded to my crying with, "Cindy, do as this doctor and nurse ask. They need to look at you. They are not going to hurt you."

With that, I reluctantly agree to take off my clothes.

"Mrs. Herb, this will only take a few minutes. If you can stand over here, I'll talk to you after we are done." The doctor pointed to an area right beside the table, within reach of me. Obligingly, my mom stepped to the side as the nurse helped me slip out of my clothes, while the doctor stood at the head of the table with his back turned.

The entire time, I was crying. The nurse covered me with the sheet, instructing me to lie on my back. Covered only with a thin sheet, I was otherwise completely naked all over again.

"Ok, sweetie, I want you to slide down here," she said. She was referring to the end of the table, where those metal arms were located. I was extremely apprehensive, but I managed to shift my body down. I started to tremble. The next thing I knew, the nurse grabbed first one foot, then the other, inserting each of them into the upright, metal arms.

Completely terrified, instinctively I repeated the course of action I had done with my rapist; I clenched my eyes closed. I did not want to see. I knew another male figure was going to invade me. And this time, my mother approved it.

"OK doctor, she's ready. I have her in the stirrups."

With the go-ahead from the nurse that I was prepared, the doctor stepped around from the head of the table to the foot of the table. I heard him sit down on a squeaky seat.

"Her panties are bloody," the nurse blurted out.

I heard him respond back, "Oh, OK. Let us see here. Her hymen might be broken."

The sound of rubber gloves being popped onto the doctor's hands boomed in my head.

"Open your legs wider, Cindy," he says to me.

I was thinking, *Oh my God! No! Is he kidding?* I complied, but obviously not up to his standards, for he took his hands and pried my knees still further apart. I felt as though I was on display.

I heard further squeaking. I could feel something warm on my exposed vaginal area as he stretched me open. Later, I would figure out the cause of the warm sensation. He used a strong spotlight, allowing him to see as he worked.

"Cindy, this may hurt a little bit."

He paused for a moment. I could sense him inspecting my body. He was just sitting there, staring at my naked bottom. I did not even know what a vagina or hymen was at that age.

My mother had not told me about the facts of life. She felt uncomfortable discussing sex. Whenever one of us asked her where babies came from, her typical response was, "Nature has its ways." She never did teach any of us about the birds and the bees. She left us to our own devices. After all, her parents taught her the way. Sex was not considered a topic of discussion, doing so was taboo. When we reached our teens, the Catholic school we attended offered their version of sex education classes, which included a healthy view of abstinence. My mother seemed overjoyed to be off the hook for instructing us about the facts of life.

So there I was in the hospital, lying flat, out on a cold table, like a fish ready to be gutted. Was this day ever going to end?

I heard the nurse ask the doctor, "Do you need the speculum?"

"Yes. Her hymen is broken. Give me the speculum."

My mother would not have been my mother if she had not said her stock three words at this moment, but she did.

"Oh my God," she exclaimed, as if it were her own hymen that was torn.

All of a sudden, I felt the doctor inserting some cold, metal object inside me. He said, "Hold on, Cindy," and then I felt pressure and pain. He was opening my vagina wider with a primitive instrument that he had just inserted inside my body. Talk about invasion; I was wide open and spotlighted. Were they going to take pictures next? My mind was freaking. I thought, *Please stop*. But he did not.

"Give me a swab; we need to take some specimens here. The police want us to collect any semen or hair." It felt like he was scraping the inside my body.

"Oouuww, that hurts," I yelled out.

"I'm almost done," my torturer replied. I felt him extract the metal contraption from my body. I thought we were done, but I was wrong again.

The doctor thrust his fingers into my vagina and anal cavity. I moaned in pain, opening my eyes only to see him standing over me. He pressed hard on my abdomen.

"I'm sorry, this will only take a few more seconds," he said rather clinically.

Finally, he removed his fingers, patting me on the abdomen as if to say "good job." I felt like saying "terrible job" to him.

"OK, we are all done," he said in a nonchalant way. He draped the sheet back over my exposed body.

The nurse had been standing idly by his side the entire time, handing him tools. My mom, who was parked just to the side of the table, had her head turned away when he hard-pressed my abdomen. I had noticed my mom's obvious lack of interest, when I had opened my eyes.

She now glanced up, expressionless, and asked the doctor, "Did he get her because her shorts were too tight?"

Is this my fault? I wondered.

The doctor answered, "Well, I don't know about that." Evading her bizarre question, he continued with his clinical analysis, "But her hymen was broken, so there definitely was penetration. Her panties are bloody. She will probably be sore. However, she should be OK. We will talk to the police about anything we have found. You can take her home as soon as she gets dressed."

He turned to the nurse and said, "She can get dressed now."

Finished, he promptly left the room.

I wondered why they did not check my mouth. I thought they would have inspected it from the smell alone. Nobody asked, and I was not about to offer to tell them. The hellacious incident with the man's Peter was too gross. As far as my parents, the police, and doctor knew, the perpetrator had only vaginally raped me. I was too embarrassed and afraid to reveal the entire, ugly episode.

Chapter 13

Cleanliness Is Next to Godliness

It turned out that July 31, 1966, was a very busy day in the Herb household. Not only did my parents wake to find out that a man had raped me, but a reporter from one of the city newspapers was set to interview my oldest brother Tommy that same day. Tommy had been mowing yards all summer long. One of his customers arranged the interview, due to Tommy's impressive work ethic. He was a hard worker. Tommy was earning extremely good money for someone only twelve years old and in the sixth grade.

I do not remember any activity surrounding Tommy when my mother and I arrived home from the hospital. However, I am sure he was preparing for the interview, even though it was not until later that afternoon. I know my brother well, and he, more than likely, was very excited.

Unfortunately, the only things I recall on returning were the actions of my mother. The minute we walked into the house, she marched me into the bathroom, rather indifferently, and drew the bathwater. She stayed there dispassionately until the tub filled with water. She then instructed me to get in, telling me to "wash," at which time she abruptly left the room. It was still quite early in the morning, our bathroom was small and dark, and she did not even bother to switch on the light. She left me sitting alone with my thoughts in the dark, cold room. I began to weep quietly.

"Nobody cares," ran through my mind, along with, "My mother is mad at me. I must have done something bad."

All my life, God has sent angels to uplift me during my most difficult trials. People are angels, even if they do not know it. You may be surprised which angel is sent your way. This was one of those times.

My sister Terry, who irritated me on most occasions, slipped into the bathroom while I was sitting there crying. I had been in the bathroom for at least fifteen minutes by myself. Terry knelt beside the tub and wrapped her loving arms around me. She just hugged me and said, "Don't worry, Cindy. Everything will be alright."

Terry gave me the emotional support I lacked from my mother. I will never forget that moment as long as

I live. I am so thankful Terry came to me, not just as a benefit for me, but also, to allow her the opportunity to help heal someone.

Little did I know, that while I was locked away inside the bathroom "washing," my mother was just outside the door executing damage control, as she probably saw it in her mind's eye. At least, this was how I perceived the whole matter. It was probably in reaction to something Mother had said that prompted Terry to come bolting into the bathroom to see me. She probably did not agree with Mother's stance on the subject, and wanted to take matters into her own hands. After all, Terry was feisty at fourteen years old. She was also the oldest sibling and was accustomed to mothering the rest of us while my parents were working during the day. Of course, I did not care if Terry's motives were altruistic or not, I was just glad to see her.

"How's she doing?"

It was my dad. He was standing in the hall when my mother initially stepped out of the bathroom.

"She'll be alright. We just have to forget this whole mess. Where's Mary?"

Directly across the hall from the bathroom was our little makeshift bedroom/dining room. Mary's twin bed was next to the wall adjacent to the hall. On the other side of that wall was my brothers' room. My mother and father had a clear view of her from their vantage point in the hall. My sister was lying on her bed, curled on her side with her hands over her face as if to mask it.

My mother, barely shutting the bathroom door, was about to head over to her when Daddy stopped her to speak. He suddenly blurted out, "If they want her to testify, she is definitely going to testify, in court, against that son of a bitch! Do you understand?"

"Do you really think that will be necessary? After all, we need to forget the whole thing. The police said she probably could not point the guy out anyway. What good would it do?"

Obviously, Daddy could not get over his anger. "I want him to get what is coming to him, that's what!"

"They haven't even found the guy. Let's wait until then." With that statement, I could hear their footsteps as she and my dad walked away, heading into the other room.

On the other side of the bathroom door, I heard every word of their conversation. I felt colder, more scared now. *Testify?* I knew exactly what that meant. My mother liked watching Perry Mason on TV. From the program, I had witnessed how lawyers made people sit in a box next to a judge, requiring they tell the truth. I knew a whole bunch of people would be present in the courtroom, all of them staring at me.

I could not tell them about what that man did to me. I did not even know if I could remember what he looked like. *Oh God! Help! Why did we have that stupid paper route?* I did not ever want to throw papers again! And especially, if the police had not found the man. *What would happen if he came after me again? What would happen if he tried to get Mary? Who would protect us?*

Mary was wide awake, but deep in thought, when my mother came up to her and sat on the bed. My sister was wondering what had happened that morning. She was confused. She knew something bad had occurred, she could tell by the interrogation from the police and the atmosphere in the house. Daddy was in an uproar, and Mom was shutdown and unnerved.

"Mary, I need to talk to you." Mary sat up on the edge of the bed, next to Mother. "Under no circumstances, are you ever to discuss what happened today with anyone, and especially not with Cindy. Is that clear?"

Mary was stunned. "But I don't even know what happened! What happened to Cindy?"

Abruptly, my mother said, "Nothing. She'll be better off if we don't talk about it." With those words, my mother strode into Terry's room to have a chat with her. She also made a point to speak with Tommy. She knew better than to bother Daddy just yet. Better let him cool off first.

Terry was still in the bathroom with me when my mother returned from making the rounds. No doubt, my mother had just finished talking to Tommy.

"Terry, let me talk to Cindy," she said.

Obediently, Terry exited the room.

"Okay, let's get you out of this tub and get you dressed. I will not make you go to church this morning because you have had a rough morning. But you and I will go to mass at five thirty."

I was crying and her words upset me further. "I don't want to go to mass! Can't I stay home, just once, from church?"

"No. Now is when you need to go to church. You will feel better if you attend church. You will see. Let us get you something to eat. Okay? Now stop that crying."

As I was trying to do as she ordered, she helped me get dressed, keeping me in the bathroom until my tears subsided. Not once did she hug me or tell me she loved me. Not once did she let me know that I need not worry. Not once did she try to quiet my fears by letting me know that things would be okay. She just wanted me to be quiet.

When I emerged from the bathroom, my whole world had changed. I could tell everyone was looking at me strangely. Only my mother, father, Terry, and Tommy understood the full extent of the gross affair. Although

Mary did not know all the details, she knew something terrible had occurred. I staggered over to the breakfast nook, and my mother set a bowl of cereal before me.

Each family member passed by, slowing inspecting me, looking for the flaw. No one said a word. They just stared. Although my stomach was spinning, I put my head down and ate; I could not bear their burning eyes. I finished as quickly as I could, and then I went and found comfort in my bed.

Not long after that day, no one ever spoke of my rape again. When I mentioned "the man," Mother swiftly changed the subject. It was a taboo subject in our house. I initially had feared someone was going to ask about the man's Peter, wanting details. Although the rape was despicable, the Peter in my mouth was very wicked. I did not know if I would ever be able to speak of it, but I had nothing to worry about. I quickly learned it was bad to discuss "the man" and suppressed the whole incident for almost thirty years.

Chapter 14

No Hope

In the meantime, life went on. Tommy had his interview with the reporter as planned. The newspaper had never interviewed anyone in our family. My dad was especially proud of his oldest son. Despite the terrible things that had happened to me that day, it appeared to be a thrilling day for the remainder of my family. I felt isolated from the excitement experienced by the rest of the family and all alone.

Late in the afternoon, there was a knock on our door for the second time that day. However, my parents were expecting this knock. The female reporter showed up with a photographer from the morning paper she represented. They weren't from the paper that Mary and I circulated, they were from a competing paper. When she arrived, the entire family rallied around, getting in on the commotion. That is, all except my younger sister Jeanne, who had been sick all day with a stomachache, and me.

The reporter sat down with Tommy to interview him. Afterwards she and the photographer wanted to take pictures of Tommy with his lawnmower. For reasons unknown to my parents at the time, they wanted all the kids in the picture, not just Tommy. However, by the time they were ready to snap the picture, my mother had carted Jeanne and me off to church for the five thirty service.

When the article and photo came out in Monday's paper, Jeanne and I were thus absent from the photo, with a mere mention of such exclusion. In the photo, Tommy was in the foreground, kneeling next to his brand-new, power lawnmower. Behind him stood Mary and Paul, and seated on the steps of the front porch was Terry, holding my baby sister Patty, who held her doll. The caption under the photo read, "Tommy admires new mower as, from left, Mary, 10, Paul, 6, Patty, 4, and Terry, 14 look on. Absent are Jeanne, 5, and Cindy, 9."

Ironically, the caption under the article was a direct commentary on my life since I was a baby. I was absent from this picture, just as I had been absent from the festivities in the kitchen when I was a baby, trying to free myself from that crib. This would prove to be a recurring subject in my life, being separated and all alone.

As for that newspaper article, it was not until it came out on page one of Section A of the paper the next morning, that my parents realized why the reporter had insisted all the children be included in the photograph with Tommy. My dad happened to be unemployed at the time, which turned out to be an unfortunate set of circumstances. The reporter spun the piece as if Tommy was completely supporting the family. Obviously, the article would "play" better, if more children were in the photograph; so as many kids as possible were included when the reporter set the picture up the day before. The paper made sure that all seven names were captioned under the photo so the public knew how many children Tommy was supposedly supporting. It was all too sad.

Even though my dad was temporarily unemployed, my mother had worked since I was about five or six years of age and never stopped. We had some sort of income coming into the household from her. I do not know if my brother supplemented her income. Maybe he did. That was between my parents and Tommy.

I only know what my mother told me about that article. She said that after it was printed, she and my dad started receiving terrible hate mail. People wrote her and inquired how she could "lie in bed and have all those kids and then expect them to support you, you lazy bitch."

One woman questioned my mother's Catholic faith, which really shook my mother to the core. The woman wrote, "I am Catholic and call myself a Christian, and I would never live off my children the way you are doing. You should be ashamed of yourself."

Between my rape and that article, my mother seemed to go into a deep depression. My mother and father had their share of fights, like any other married couple. However, my parents' fighting seemed to escalate during our stay at 4319 Bowser, centering mostly around financial issues. All of us used to scatter whenever they would start to scream.

Forever etched in my memory is one such battle. My mother was very upset with my dad. They had been arguing for some time, and apparently, she was not making any headway with her point of view. In the heat of the argument, we heard, "I can't live like this anymore! I wish I were dead. I'm just going to kill myself!" With that statement, she stormed out of the living room and into their bedroom.

Although she was trying to get my dad's attention, the only interest she gained was my six other siblings' and mine. As quickly as we had scattered, we now congregated in the hall with our eyes fixed firmly in the direction of her room.

Within seconds, she reappeared, brushing us aside and tromping into the bathroom, carrying one of Daddy's ties. She wrapped it around the shower-curtain rod and proceeded to hang herself. It was deliberate and cold. All the while, my siblings and I were pleading, screaming, and bawling, "No Momma! Please stop! Oh Daddy, please stop her!" It was an awful sight.

Of course, nothing ever fazed my dad. He just said, "Oh shit." Then he would march out of the room. I knew this would be one of those times. As my mother stepped off the edge of the tub, trying to suspend her entire body by the neck, the tie slipped out of the knot. She fell on her butt to the tile floor. My dad just stood there in the doorway, watching, and then he barked, "Oh shit. Damn you, woman!" After reprimanding her, he turned his back and strutted away. Perhaps he did not think she was sincere in her effort.

My dad's comment seemed to make my mother even madder. She did not even acknowledge all of her children beseeching her to stop. She simply picked herself off the floor and, with a determined look, headed back into her bedroom. Within seconds, she emerged once more. This time, she produced one of my dad's flimsy belts.

Each of us was shouting in unison, begging her to reconsider. "No Momma! Please do not kill yourself! Do not leave us! Stop! Oh no! Do not do it, Momma! Pleeeease! Daddy, come back!" Still she ignored us. While we were all gathered around, she looped the tie around the curtain rod.

"It's no use, kids. Your Daddy does not care, and he does not love me. He doesn't want me around here."

"We want you, Momma," we screamed.

She didn't care. She stepped off the tub, and there was a loud crash.

"What the hell is going on?" Daddy reappeared, in response to our screams, and was standing in the hall. On her second attempt, the entire curtain rod came tumbling down, hitting my mother on the head. The belt held firm, but the rod could not support the weight of her body.

"Momma. Oh Momma! Thank God you are okay!" All seven of us encircled with our arms outstretched, crowding the small space. Hugging her at the same time, we all cried together. She appeared to have lost her thunder at last. The bump on the noggin was perhaps the final defeating blow.

"Goddamn you!" was the last response from my dad as he fumed back into the other room, ready to drink himself into a beer stupor while smoking endless cigarettes. Fortunately for me and my other siblings, despite her best efforts, my mother was unable to hang herself that day.

Chapter 15

Making a Deal

I was adamant about quitting the paper route. However, everybody ignored my wish. My mother erased my rape from the consciousness of the household. It was my "duty" to go on as if nothing had happened. I endured.

Although my mother did her best to hush the entire household, she was not that successful at quieting my dad. He eventually was silenced, but not by her. It was by the fear of me.

Several days had passed since my horrific ordeal. One early afternoon, Daddy, who was not working, asked me to get him another beer as we watched TV. It was summertime, and most of the time the children in our family were outside playing. Today was no exception. Depressed from Sunday's trauma, I stayed inside. I was the only child in the house.

Before I knew it, Daddy asked me to follow him. We headed towards my parents' bedroom. As soon as we were inside the door, he closed it behind us. The bedroom doors were always left open in our house, so my gut told me something was wrong. But I let the feeling slide, considering this was my dad. Everything had to be okay.

But then, he surprised and shocked me. He pulled back the sheet, slid into bed, and instructed me to lie beside him. Alarms were going off in my head. The last two times I was lying next to a man, each invaded me. *Oh my God! Could this actually be happening again?*

Despite my fear, I obeyed his command. He was my father. What else could I do but obey? To go against my father was not a smart thing to do in our family. He was loud and could be very mean. He could make us feel very small. He did not hit, although he would raise his fist as if he were going to punch us. Because of his vicious comments, my mother often made the comment, "I'd rather he hit me instead of using spiteful words, because they are so much more painful."

"Cindy, I want you to know what a penis looks and feels like, so nobody can ever take advantage of you again. So I want you to touch my penis." *Was he crazy? Didn't he understand I already knew about that vile body part?* I did not like this at all.

"No, Daddy!"

He moved closer, and the pungent smell of beer and cigarettes invaded my senses. He had not shaved today. He was gross. It reminded me of the previous Sunday's image. I was getting sick.

"Don't worry, just rub against me, and then I'll show you what it looks like. Then you can go." Daddy appeared oblivious to my fear.

Before I could react, my dad grabbed my lower body, pulling me across his abdomen. He then rubbed his penis across my vagina. In a soft whisper, he said, "Whatever you do, don't tell Mommy. She would not understand this. I'm just trying to protect you."

I began weeping. Maybe he did understand my hesitation, but he just did not care. I wanted out, but I knew I did not dare leave. I wondered when he was going to show me his penis and if he is going to raid me the way the other men did. *Are all men the same?* Before I could finish the thought, he quietly said, "Cindy, I want you to look here." With that, he lifted the sheet and pulled down his boxer shorts, exposing himself to me.

Now I understood what the man was referring to when he said, "Do you know what a Peter is?" I recalled him saying, "It's that thing that hangs between your dad's legs." At the time, I did not want to think about what my dad had in his pants. Now, thanks to my father, I knew for sure. I was right. It was not a pretty picture.

"Make sure you don't tell Mommy. Okay?" My father was getting nervous now. "I just want to make sure you are protected. That is why I am doing this. Do you understand?"

I did not understand. As far as I was concerned, if my parents wanted to protect us, they would never have let us go out by ourselves on Sunday mornings.

An opportunity presented itself, and I took it.

"I'm scared to throw papers on Sunday morning. Can't you or Momma go out with Mary and me on Sunday mornings?"

"I'll talk to Mommy. One of us will go with you. If I do, will you keep our secret?" I had him under the barrel.

"Yes, Daddy. Can I go now?"

He let me go, and I jumped out of bed. I raced as quickly as I could down the hall and into the bathroom, shutting the door behind me. I leaned over the toilet and started to vomit.

After that day, my father began accompanying Mary and I on our Sunday route. The back end of our family car replaced the old, noisy shopping cart. He drove our Rambler station wagon slowly down the street as Mary and I delivered the newspapers door to door. I felt I had won the battle and would be safe from other men. In return, my father's secret was safe.

On many Sundays after we finished the route, my father took us for breakfast at Lucas B&B, a neighborhood restaurant on Oak Lawn Avenue. This treat was conceivably a reward for my silence, especially since money was tight.

Mary was not aware of my conversation with my father or our deal. She always thought he began escorting us because my parents wanted to protect us. As far as I know, they still would have let us go out by ourselves had I not asked my father to ride along.

Why do I think this? They continued to let us collect our paper fees late into the evening. If they really were trying to protect us, they would have stopped us from going out at night by ourselves, collecting those fees. But they never did. I had not made that deal.

Chapter 16

The Strength of Protection

It is a scary thing to be only nine years old and realize you are all by yourself in the world, with no one to protect you. Sadly, my father is one of the people I needed protection from. My mother could not protect me, and—what is even worse—she would not protect me.

Since the rape and Daddy's major indiscretion, I was on guard around my father. I kept his secret, but I was not about to let it happen again. I never gave him the opportunity to catch me alone. I tried to stay out of the house when he was home. At the very least, I made darn sure others were present when he was around.

I prevailed. My father never tried his fiendish act with me again. Whether this was because I never gave him the chance or because of the fear of recrimination, I will never know.

In the summertime, it was easy to stay outdoors. The City of Dallas Parks and Recreation Department operated a series of neighborhood parks and swimming pools, which we children frequented most days. When we were not earning money in some creative way or spending it, we were usually participating in some activity at the park.

One morning, just a few weeks after I my rape, Mary and I went to the park. When it came time to throw papers in the afternoon, I was in the middle of a game of checkers with another kid at the park. So Mary picked up her bicycle and rode home, leaving me to follow her as soon as I was done with my match. However, as soon as I completed the game, I was astounded to find my bike had vanished.

The parks program had a standard practice of keeping a couple of chaperones at each park location, usually one male and one female. This was the case at our park. When my bike turned up missing, I went to one of these group supervisors and asked for help.

The park we hung around was located at an elementary school called Stephen J. Hay. It had rather extensive grounds, so children could play during recess and lunchtime when school was in session. Within its perimeter, there was a baseball diamond, as well as a swimming pool. Mike, one of the park chaperones, and I searched the entire grounds of the school and park but could not find the bike. Mike decided to call the police, who took a report and sent me on my way.

I was in a hurry to get home that day because Mary was waiting for me to help throw those papers. I was late because of the commotion with my bike, but she would have no idea what had transpired and would likely be upset with me. It was only a few blocks from the park to our house, so I made haste as soon as the police made their report.

Since Stephen J. Hay was located on Gilbert Avenue, between Prescott and Herschel Avenues, I would hike down Herschel Avenue past Holland Avenue, continuing on to Bowser Avenue to get home. It was only another short, half-block stretch from the corner of Herschel and Bowser to our house.

As I began my fast stride down Herschel, a car came into view, catching my attention. It headed towards me down the street, traveling at a very slow pace. I could see what appeared to be a middle-aged man driving the car. His car was big, blue, and an older-model vehicle. The man was staring at me.

The hairs rose on the back of my neck; I was suddenly very uncomfortable. I looked around, searching for anyone else on the street. There was no one. Before I knew it, he was pulling up beside me. He rolled his window down. I did not deter from my mission; I kept moving. He stuck his head out the window, and I heard him ask as I continued along, "Do you need a ride, sweetie?" I ignored him and kept walking, my pace increasing faster with each heartbeat.

Panicking, I started feeling as if someone was going to attack me all over again. I was so close to home. How could this be happening? It was daylight, for God's sake! What was this guy thinking? He was not even going in the same direction as I was.

At least Mary would try to protect me, I thought. As I moved forward, I could hear him put his car into gear and drive away. Oh, thank you, God. I am safe.

I kept walking. I tried to calm down a bit, thinking I was just being too paranoid. After all, why should I mistrust this man? He probably was only trying to help me. Right? He could see I was in a hurry by the speed of my step. Yeah, that must be it.

I was wrong again. The man had driven around the block and, as I was about to reach Bowser Avenue, he instantly materialized at my side. I was shocked. I had not even heard him drive up because I was in such a hurried state to get my butt home, due to both my tardiness and his traumatizing appearance.

As he approached me from behind, the driver's side door was the one closest to the sidewalk, so he was nearer to me than before. He swung open the door before I had a chance to respond. As he did so, I saw he was sitting there, completely naked from the waist down. He smiled a dastardly grin. My face went ashen.

He asked, "Do you know what this is?"

Without hesitation, I started to run, intently listening with every step I took for the sound of his car approaching. Was he still following me? I only had a half block more to go and then I would be safe inside my house. Or would I? If Daddy were home, that might be questionable. I knew I had to take the risk. Oh God! Help me!

I reached our house; the papers had just arrived. Mary was folding them. "Cindy, where have you been? I thought you'd be home before now." Then, she realized I did not have my bike. "Where's your bicycle?"

I was still out of breath from running, but I respond. "Somebody stole it. That's why I'm late. And I'm scared! Some man has been following me from the park, and I thought he was going to get me."

Mary looked disturbed. "What? Are you sure?"

Even though my mother had told my sister never to discuss the subject of my rape on that ill-fated Sunday morning, Mary had ignored her. She could never comprehend the reason my mother wanted her to keep quiet. She and I had always spoken openly and freely about everything, like best friends. Mary felt this was no exception. She wanted to know what happened. She thought it was her right. After all, I was not the only one left out there all alone in the dark. So was she. Without our mother's knowledge, she had asked me, secretly, what occurred that Sunday morning. She knew if I wanted to, I would tell her.

Mary waited until the day after the rape, when my mother was away at work, to speak with me. Calmly, she sat down on my bed and asked, "Cindy, what happened yesterday?"

I did not give her the details. It was all too painful. I simply told her about the man asking me to help him find his cat and explained, "He got me instead."

"What do you mean?" she asked.

"He just did some horrible things to me." It was all I could say.

"Momma doesn't want me to talk about this with you, but I had to ask," she said.

"I know. I was going to tell you anyway. I was worried he was going to get you too. He told me if I said anything, he would hurt me again and maybe hurt you." It was the last thing I said to her that day. We never spoke of the rape again, until I was an adult.

So Mary fully understood my terror, weeks later, when I said, "He was going to get me," after the man in the car exposed himself to me.

I responded to her question when she asked if I was sure about the incident. "Yes, he drove up and opened his door, and he was naked!"

I spared her the gory details of him asking me if I knew about his wiener-shaped, lower body part. I figured she did not need to know that. Why bring her into that immoral mindset? I knew exactly about the Peter, penis, or whatever you wanted to call it, because of the horrific circumstances experienced a few short weeks beforehand. Yes, dear sister, I was quite certain this dirty old man was up to no good.

Mary now went into protector mode, something my parents did not seem to be able to accomplish. "Where did this happen?"

I pointed in the direction of Herschel Avenue and responded, "Right down the block on Hershel, he drove up in his car and wanted to give me a ride. I kept walking, and then he turned around and came up from behind me, but I did not know it. He just opened his door and he was naked. Then I ran all the way home. I hope he did not see where we live. I'm so scared."

The entire time I was speaking, Mary was looking up and down the street for any cars, but none were around. She said, "Let's go tell Daddy."

Mary and my father always had a good relationship. She had no reason to mistrust him as I had.

When I explained to my father what had happened, he surprised me by appearing very upset. I also explained that my bicycle was missing, apparently stolen. He called the police and, before long, they arrived at the house.

In just a few short weeks, it was the third time in my life where someone called the police because of me: once for my rape, second for my bicycle, a third time for this situation.

As the police took the report, they also noted the stolen bicycle report which had been made on the same day. The officers took my description of the car and the man. They said they would keep a watchful eye on the neighborhood, looking for him. In the meantime, they explained to me that it was necessary for me to get the license plate number of his car if I saw him again.

Just a few hours later, the police found my bicycle. They located it in an open breezeway of an eight-unit apartment building on the corner of Herschel Avenue and Holland Avenue. I had walked right past this apartment on my way home from the park that very afternoon.

My parents wondered how on earth the police had even discovered the bike. The police told them that they received an anonymous phone call. Someone at the small apartment building saw a bike matching the description I had given to the police. Outfitted with a double wire basket, once used to throw papers and situated over the rear tire, my bicycle had unique features. This made it easy for the officers to identify.

When the police drove up to our house to produce my lost bicycle, Mary and I had just returned from our paper route. I listened intently from the comfort of my bed, just a few feet away from the living area, as the police spoke to my father. My mother was not yet home from work. The police told my father that they had suspected that the man who was following me had probably stolen my bike. He, more than likely, intended to use the bike as bait, to try to lure me into one of those apartments. They discovered during their investigation that a man matching the description I had given lived in one of the units at the apartment building.

"Well, are you going to arrest that man?" my father demanded.

"We spoke to him, but he already has an alibi that cannot be substantiated at this time. At this point, it is a case of her word against his. She's got her bike back. We do not think he will try it again. He knows we are watching him."

I was only nine years old but growing older by the minute. I did not need to hear anymore. I knew what this meant. I was on my own.

From that point on, Mary and I threw our papers, ever heedful of the cars passing by. I was never very far from her. Weeks passed and nothing happened. My guard came down, and I thought life might be normal again. It was the end of August and still very hot. School was just about to begin. The park had closed for the summer, and we found other things to occupy our time until classes resumed.

I had a friend, who lived less than one block away, who had recently been severely burned. The fire took place in the winter. She went into the bathroom in the morning with a blanket wrapped around her, as she was half asleep. The bathroom was small and crowded. On the floor, close to one window, a gas-flamed heater stood. Without her knowing it, her blanket had draped over the tiny heater as she staggered into the room.

Within seconds, the blanket ignited, turning her into a ball of fire. She screamed, sending her father flying into the room. He attempted to put her out by rolling her on the floor. The family also responded by dousing them both with water to extinguish the flames. However, the damage was done. She ended up having severe burns over most of her body and face. Her father burned his hands trying to put out the flames that engulfed his daughter. It was a terrible tragedy.

One afternoon, I decided to pay my friend a visit. I asked Mary if she wanted to go, but she was busy making some tissue-paper flowers and wanted to finish her project. I thought about it for a moment and decided to go on my own. It was only a short walk to her house—less than one block.

From our house to the corner of Wycliff Avenue, there was only one apartment building and a house. I had to cross this street and then stroll only about four houses down to my friend's house. It was simple.

I made it to her house okay and had a great visit. As I left her house, I was optimistic about life and had forgotten about all the shenanigans of the previous few weeks. I started the few steps towards home.

"Do you need a ride, sweetie?"

Oh my God! It was the middle-aged man, a second time. As I was waiting to cross Wycliff, he had come up from behind me where I was standing on the corner. Luckily, the driver's-side door was not nearest to the sidewalk.

"Leave me alone!"

He had that dastardly grin on his face again. I just knew he was once more in his car unclad.

"I'm calling the police!"

The minute he understood my intentions, he turned the corner and sped down the street. It was not until he was halfway down the street that I remembered to get his license plate number. It was too late, but it did not really matter. The whole incident caught me so off guard that I did not have the wherewithal to remember anyhow.

What did this man see in me? I hurried home. I told my parents, knowing full well, their protecting me was probably not in the cards. I would still be on my own; there was zilch my parents could do to help me.

Although my parents made another call to the police, they told my parents they really could not do anything without a license plate number. The officer also told my parents I had not been hurt. The man was only stalking me. Back then, there were no anti-stalking laws. My parent's advice to me: "Run away." My thought was: "Gee, thanks. How the heck am I supposed to outrun someone in a car?"

School started and Mary and I kept on with our paper route. Life went on. I saw the man every so often, following me in his car. Sometimes he was in a light brown car instead of a blue car. He must have had two vehicles. I never bothered to say anything more to my parents. Why bother?

When Mary was with me, he did not approach. Instead, he would just drive down the street. I never said anything to her. Why worry her? But if I were by myself, he tried to get my attention every time. He never attempted to get out of his car.

After awhile, I realized he was just some pervert who wanted to show me his sick body. Watched and followed, time on this earth passed, day after day, month after month, year after year, with me always on my guard. No one ever really knew the torment I was bearing. When I was in my teens, he finally stopped following me. He must have either died or moved. But I had endured until everything stopped in my late teens and life was good once more.

My mother had a saying whenever there was a death in the family: "Bad news comes in threes." Well, she was not kidding. Here was a numbers connection in my life that I would later identify as significant. Three different men had validated that number within a short time with three horrendous acts: a rapist, my father, and a pervert in a car.

Yes, death comes in threes, but there is rebirth afterwards. I was not aware of it at the time, but I would not come back to life until I made changes in my life many years later.

Chapter 17

The Stuff We Are Made Of

Every other person in my immediate family was of normal weight, but I became fat. Of course, I think there were a lot of contributing factors to this trend. For one thing, my maternal grandmother was a rather large woman, and I favored her. Photographs have confirmed this. I also look similar to my mother's sister, who was also plump. However, genes alone were not the sole contributor to my weight gain.

When I was born, I was about the same weight as my other siblings. More or less, we all weighed six to seven pounds, except for my brother Tommy and my sister Jeanne who both weighed over eight pounds.

As a toddler, I had more baby fat than any of my brothers or sisters had, but I was not fat. But my dad started calling me his little "Fatstuff." He also called my sister Mary, who had smaller bones than I did, by another derogatory name. We both hated these names. My mother never tried to stop him from calling us by these unsavory labels. I think she thought they were terms of endearment. Mary and I thought otherwise.

By the time I reached kindergarten, I was of normal size. As a matter of fact, Mary and I looked so much alike that relatives and friends often remarked to my mother that they did not know she had twins. She always had to correct them, telling them we were fourteen months apart in age.

This was of no consequence to my father; he still called me Fatstuff, despite the fact that I was not fat. At least, not until after a strange man raped me, a doctor pillaged me, and my father sexually fondled me. After these sordid events, I did actually begin to gain weight.

On the same day as my rape, my mother inadvertently set me up for fatness subconsciously. She did this by trying to pacify me with food, saying, "Let's get you something to eat," right after I had been raped. She sat me in front of a bowl of cereal after I had bathed in the tub and did not let me up until I finished that food. After that day, I subconsciously associated not eating with being bad.

When I hit puberty, my father finally stopped calling me Fatstuff. Instead, he decided to humiliate me even more; "Two-Ton" was my new nickname. At the time, I was enrolled in a home economics class at Rusk Junior

High School. A class assignment was to make a dress. One day, I was sewing the dress and he happened to be there. He watched for several minutes and then put in his two cents.

"Why don't you just take a potato sack and put it on, Two-Ton?"

The only response I could muster was, "Oh, Daddy!" Of course, because I am left-handed, he did call me "Lefty" every so often, and I was thankful for that reprieve.

The bad thing about a parent who has incorrect behaviors is that they show their children that these responses are okay, then children emulate the behavior. This was the case in our family. My dad egged us on when we used those same names for each other. He gave offensive names to Mary, Jeanne, and I. As the years passed, every child in our family had some kind of disparaging nickname made up by some member of the family, due to my father's initial influence.

Therefore, I don't think it was my oldest sister's fault when she once said to me, "I don't want you wobbling down the aisle," when we were discussing her upcoming wedding. She had taken me aside to inform me that I was too fat. She wanted me to go on a diet. I remember thinking she was out of her head. At the time, I weighed 140 pounds.

Years later, while participating in a supervised diet program, I learned that the optimal weight for someone with my height and bone structure was between 135 and 146 pounds. So, I had not been overweight. Terry's misconstrued concept of my body, due to my father's training, made her think I was larger. I do not blame her; culpability rests with him and Mother.

Why do I blame my mother? She was so obtuse to the situation; all of the name-calling happened under her seemingly comatose presence. Not once did she try to correct the problem or stop it. After all, most mothers usually offer support and encouragement for their children. I didn't have that.

It was not as if she did not know about nutrition. My mother, in her vanity, was always on a diet. She was concerned about Mary's weight, because she thought she was too skinny and tried to get her to eat more. She may have worried about Mary's health, because my sister was anemic; she insisted Mary take iron supplements.

But she never once placed me on a diet or talked to me about dieting. When I was older, I placed myself on diets. When I told her I was going on a diet, she eagerly went on it with me. Not because she wanted me to lose weight, it was the other way around. She was wishing to lose weight herself. My mother was just happy to have a partner to keep her on track. Why wasn't she concerned for my health the way she was concerned for others in our family?

Over the years, she often commented to me that I was the sickliest sibling in the family, but she never tried to fix the problem. It was as though she just wanted to ignore the problem. It was the same as she had always done since I was raped, disregarding my welfare, hushing the family after the incident. She closed her eyes to the rape completely. I was a constant reminder to her of tribulations in her past. She did not want to deal with them; therefore, I suffered.

The lack of appropriate nutritional support was not the only thing that bothered me. My little sister Jeanne was a perfect case in point. My dad had a soft spot for little girls. Maybe this was the reason God blessed him with five daughters. Each time he had a new daughter, he showered his affection on the newest arrival.

When my youngest sister, Patty, was born, he began to shun my other little sister Jeanne. This aggravated my mother tremendously. She could see the hurt in little Jeanne's eyes. She fought many of her battles with my dad over Jeanne, oftentimes creating intense arguments.

I had witnessed her nurturing nature firsthand before the rape. When I was about six years old, I recall her deciding to perm my hair. Since she dressed us similarly and cut our hair the same, she also permed Mary's hair.

Although the whole process was a stinky, time-consuming job, and I did not really like the results, I cherished it as a special time with my mom. She had shown me that she had the true character of a mother who takes care of her children. When I was raped, I think she also felt raped, and this affected her decisions about me for practically the rest of her life.

Chapter 18

Law of Attraction

Even though I started to gain weight after my rape, boys were interested in me. Despite what everyone else thought in my family, I did not actually balloon to an enormous size until I reached adulthood. So, to others, I was attractive.

My first kiss from a boy was especially memorable. I was ten years old. At the time, my brother Tommy had a friend who I thought was genuinely cute. He was a year older than my thirteen-year-old brother was. I cannot even remember his name, although I have repeatedly tried to recall it. I think I was so affected by the kiss that I blocked it out.

Anyway, Tommy's friend was over, goofing off with him one day. My best friend Lynn was also there to visit me. Lynn was a thin girl with mid-length, blonde hair, and my older brother thought she was pretty. All four of us were standing out on the front lawn, waiting for her mother to pick her up. It was summertime, right before dinner on a Wednesday night.

I know it was Wednesday because my mother was cooking dinner. Wednesday was her day off from work and she customarily cooked dinner on any day she was off from work. That included Sunday. On every other day of the week, I prepared dinner.

It was nice to have my mother home on Wednesdays, especially as added protection from my father. My friend was visiting this particular day, since her mother would not allow her to visit unless my mother was home.

As we stood on the lawn, I heard Tommy's friend say to my brother, "Give it to the cute one," catching our attention. Lynn and I momentarily stopped our conversation and turned our focus to Tommy and his friend. They were grinning. We did not know what they were discussing. I assumed his friend was referring to Lynn, since I knew Tommy thought she was pretty and she looked older than I did. Besides, my self-esteem was quite low due to the unfortunate events that had happened in my life thus far, and I could not imagine he was talking about me. Lynn's mother arrived, and I said goodbye and they drove away.

"Hey, you wanna play kick-the-can?" Tommy asked.

Since our family was rather large, it was a routine occurrence to find us playing a game called kick-the-can, an urban version of hide-and-seek.

I said, "Okay, but we'd better get some other people." I knew it would be more fun if we had more than three kids.

Tommy replied, "Don't worry, we will find some more."

We both started calling out for my other siblings to join us. Several of my brothers and sisters exited the house or appeared from the backyard. We decided Tommy's friend would be "it." Tommy's friend started his countdown, and we scattered.

I ran to several places but settled on a spot behind an air-conditioning unit sticking out of a window on the other side of my next-door neighbor's house. She was an elderly woman and very sweet. She did not seem to mind the ruckus our large family continually made. I waited there patiently, listening intently, as "it" counted to fifty. I could hear him as he stood on the sidewalk, right in front of our house, " . . . forty-seven, forty-eight, forty-nine, fifty."

A chill ran down my back; it had only been one year before that I was counting these exact same numbers, as I lay naked on the grass. I quickly blocked the thought from my mind.

Without warning, I felt a hand slide up my back. I turned. It was Tommy's friend. *Oh no! He had found me. I would be out of the game.*

"You are so pretty," he said.

His remark threw me off. "No, you mean my friend, Lynn, don't you?"

He grinned and said, "No, I mean you."

I blushed as my heart began to race. He was making me uncomfortable. He moved in closer as I backed away.

In an instant, he grabbed me in his arms, thrusting his tongue deep inside my throat. It was wet and slimy, sloshing around my mouth and tongue. I pushed away. As I did, I could hear my mother calling from the front door of our house.

"Kids, it's time to eat! Get in here!"

I was glad to hear her call. Turning, I ran away, leaving Tommy's friend alone to attack someone else.

My heart was pounding so hard, I thought it was going to bounce out of my chest. I ran as quickly as I could toward our home, flying into the house, wiping the slobber off my face as I retreated. As I sat down at the table for dinner, I wondered if anyone could tell Tommy's friend had just kissed me.

Later, I told Tommy that I never wanted to see his friend again. While most girls would have loved to be the focus of such a cute admirer, I was not interested in his advances. It was too much for me to bear. Tommy's friend had not merely given me a peck on the lips. He French kissed me! I felt as though another man had invaded me all over again.

Maybe that is one reason why I have never dated very much. My first real date was in high school. I was a sophomore, and I went out with a senior, who happened to be the president of the senior class. I did not even know he liked me until the day he came up to me during lunch and asked me to the annual year-end Senior All-Night Party held at a local amusement park. I was clueless when it came to love.

At the time, I asked him if he was sure that he wanted to go with me. I could not believe it. How on earth could one of the most popular boys in school be interested in me? He was, and it was rather thrilling. So I told him I would go with him.

Curiously, my parents did not object to an all-night affair. However, I was somewhat scared. I felt myself questioning whether he would act like the other men did. Subconsciously, I wished my parents had objected. The boy was a really nice guy, and I had always enjoyed his company, but that was before I knew he liked me more than just as a friend. We would be going out all night long. The fact that it would be my first date did not help matters, instead making me only more anxious. I didn't know how I would handle a kiss, remembering my old war wounds. Despite my vacillating feelings about the evening, in the end, I continued with the date.

I left the house on my first date at about nine o'clock in the evening because the party started at eleven and ended at dawn. My date had invited another couple to go with us. After picking them up, we decided to go via his friends' car to the amusement park. My date and I rode in the back seat.

As we drove over to the park, my date began to cuddle. Most girls would welcome a warm set of arms around her body, but I was uncomfortable with his physical advances. I did not want him to think I was a baby, so I kept going with the flow and did not object, even when he started to kiss my neck and ear.

As the evening wore on, my date continued to squeeze my hand in his and embrace me affectionately while we rode the various amusement park rides. Although I wanted to evade all of his advances, I occasionally kissed him back out of guilt for not appreciating his interest. It was agonizing. I did not really think about why I was feeling this way. I did like him. I just was not fond of this particular kind of attention. Looking back on the evening, it probably was very frustrating for the poor guy, as he must have seen me as a complete tease.

Finally, the night was over. I still had one hurdle to jump, the goodnight kiss. As we pulled up to my house,

I imagined my dad sitting in the front room, waiting for me to arrive. I just knew he would hear the car and would be watching as my date opened the car door for me. By this time, the sun was rising. I was nervous as a person stepping on hot coals, as we wandered up the path to the porch. My stomach started to knot once we stopped at the front door.

Before I knew it, he stepped forward, grabbing me gently. I closed my eyes, all the while thinking of my dad watching us, the thought boring into my head as my date kissed me softly on the lips. There was no slobber and no tongue. Thank God, it was not a French kiss.

It was several days later when the boy called and asked me out a second time, but I had other plans. He must have thought I was giving him the brush off, because he never called me again. Just as well, I was not ready to date anyway.

There were a few other guys interested in me in high school, but I was extremely naive when members of the opposite sex were attracted to me. It usually took an overt gesture, such as candy for Valentine's Day or Mary informing me of their interest, before I became aware of such attentions. But though I craved love, I did not want anyone touching me. I refrained from showing any attraction to any of my suitors. Therefore, I did not date much, and when I did, it was not for long. Backing away from men became a major theme of my life.

Chapter 19

The Search for Knowledge

Instead of boys, I concentrated on other things. Straight after high school, I went to college. It seemed like the logical thing to do, especially since I did not really know what I wanted to do with my life at that point. Mary, who I always seemed to follow, talked me into going to Southern Methodist University (SMU), which is located within the Dallas city limits.

When it came to choosing a major, I haphazardly chose a degree in mathematics. I had always had an interest in numbers and excelled at math. In high school, I had an exceptional trigonometry teacher. Therefore, when I had to declare a major, mathematics seemed as good a major as any other did.

However, by my third semester, my interest began to wane. I began to question what I could do with a degree in mathematics. I knew I did not want to go into education, and I sure as heck did not want to go into engineering. I was at a crossroads. Thankfully, good fortune blessed me in this time of indecision.

My oldest sister's husband had attended SMU, graduating a few short years before I began classes with a degree in broadcast-film. He had always told me I was extremely creative and artistic. When he discovered I was contemplating changing majors, he immediately brought up the broadcast-film department. It was of no consequence to him that I had never picked up a camera in my life. Actually, it did not matter to me either. The more he spoke about it, the more it intrigued me.

So, in the fall of my sophomore year, with just a little encouragement from my brother-in-law, I switched majors. I knew I was home the minute I promenaded through the door of SMU's Meadows School of the Arts building. Never looking back on my decision, I diligently applied myself until I received a bachelor of fine arts degree two and half years later.

I made many new friends and had the time of my life, and even though I never ended up working in the broadcast-film industry, I never regretted getting that degree. Somehow, I always thought I would come back to this area of my life.

Working in the eclectic arts building had brought out a creative side to me, luring me to explore my inner connection to numbers—a feeling I had since childhood. I loved mathematics and excelled at it. Although I was no longer a mathematics major, I was still intensely interested in numbers. I wanted to step out of the box and decided to delve into more private and secret practices.

I became interested in numerology, a tradition bound by spiritual evidence, and the relationship between numbers and living things. Numerology and numerological divination were popular among early mathematicians such as Pythagoras. However, most scientists today, regard these studies as pseudo mathematics and no longer consider them part of mathematics.

Despite how most scientists currently view numerology, as I probed further into this subject, I realized it, indeed, is based upon repeatable and verifiable sources. By testing the information through a scientific approach, it is possible to validate it.

In numerology, information can be determined about a person based on two pieces of information: the full birth name (not a married name or nickname) and the date of birth. Each letter of the alphabet has a mathematical number assigned to it in numerology. Designating a number to each letter of the alphabet, you can calculate the numeric value of a person's name.

For instance, the letter a equals 1, b equals 2, c is 3, and so forth. Adding together the numeric values for letters with double digits, provides a single digit number for a letter. For example, the letter n is the 14th letter of the alphabet. To get the numeric value of this letter, you add 1 plus 4 to get 5. In this way, you can calculate a value for a person's name, or various components thereof, to ascertain different aspects of his or her chart.

As time passed, I also became interested in astrology and palmistry. My best friend and I located a monthly psychic fair in the city and began periodically attending it. I found the subjects fascinating. There appeared to be a connection between numbers, the stars or the imprints in our hands, and ourselves. We just had to be able to understand it. The more I studied, the more it interested me, as the things I discovered seemed to apply not only to others I knew, but especially to me.

Although I was deeply attracted to such phenomena, I hid this knowledge from friends and family. Raised by a mother who was a devout Catholic, I felt guilty about my interest in these supposedly occult practices. Even though the word "occult" is derived from the Latin word occultus, meaning "hidden" and referring to the "knowledge of the hidden," it has an unconstructive connotation associated with it for many individuals. I was lulled into this false assumption in my younger years that would ultimately play a role in whether I continued pursuit of these subjects. As the years passed by, I drifted away from the study of numerology and other mystical interests.

As soon as I graduated college, instead of working in the broadcasting field, I ended up securing a stable job at a professional benefits consulting firm. This was primarily because I struggled to find work in film, television, and photography for about a year after graduation, barely earning a living. Consequently, like many of my classmates, I abandoned my first love.

I went looking for a job where I could make enough money to pay the bills. Luckily, I had begun my education with mathematics as my major, and I was actually quite good at math. For that reason, I was able to obtain a well paying position using those math skills.

Part Three

Presenting the Discord

Chapter 20

Imbalance of Love

Although I had finished college and secured stable employment, I was the only child in our family who did not get married or move into an apartment before the age of twenty-five. My dad died in January 1981. Had he lived longer, I always thought I would have probably left on my own, because the fear of living with him was so disconcerting. As far as my mother was concerned, she never suggested or asked that I move out.

Looking back on it, I now think I was fooling myself. I was simply too afraid to go out and be on my own. I knew all too well the cruelty of the outside world. It was easier to live with a broken-down father, who once was a monster to me, than to face a world of unknowns.

When I was in school, I could not actually afford to live by myself, but after being hired at a professional firm, I was making very good money. I bought my own car and even helped my mother out with expenses.

Most parents kick their kids out of the house if they do not leave the roost within a reasonable time because it is healthier for them to be on their own. My dad was too sick to care about me moving out, much less anything else. However, I would have at least expected my mother to intervene and encourage me to get my own apartment. This would have been the healthy thing to do, to allow me to grow properly, but this was not the case.

Instead, she actually encouraged me to stay at home. This was especially true after my dad died. And she did not even charge me rent, even though she was on a limited income. Charging me rent would have made her life much easier.

Although I did not pay rent, I did contribute monetarily to her well-being. Of my own volition, I put a new roof on her house, bought her new furniture, re-carpeted her house, rewired her house, and painted it inside and out.

She would not have been able to afford such repairs, and I was always glad to help. After all, I was living under her roof, and I did expect to pay something for that service. I wanted our house to look nice. Without these updates, the house would have deteriorated considerably.

In 1991, I purchased a brand new car for her. She needed a car because her vehicle, a mid-1970s model, baby blue Ford Mercury Bobcat, had stopped operating.

She had another car; a 1963 faded, blue Buick sedan that she and my dad had purchased with very low mileage from a little old lady who no longer drove. However, it too was becoming unreliable.

In 1991, my mother worked as a cake decorator for Neiman Marcus. They shipped their bakery goods from the main facility, located in a huge warehouse close to downtown Dallas. Her hours were from four a.m. to noon. It was only a short ten- to fifteen-minute drive, but she had to drive through some rough neighborhoods to get there.

Until my dad got sick at the age of fifty-two, he always drove. If my dad was working and my mother needed to go somewhere, she simply rode the bus. It was only after he fell ill that she found it imperative to take a driver's license test. She was forty-eight. Since she was older when she learned to drive, she was much more flustered and anxious about it than your usual carefree teenager, and she did not like driving, so she often asked others to drive for her. That role mainly fell to me.

I had been driving her around town for almost seventeen years when I decided that she needed a reliable car, one she could use to drive herself when necessary. I was worried something bad might happen to her if her car broke down in the trip to or from work. She drove to work at about three thirty a.m., and there were very few people on the street who could assist her if she was in trouble. In 1991, cell phones were not as prevalent as they are today. She could not just pick up a phone and call for help. Ironically, I was more worried about her welfare in the wee morning hours, than she had been for me some twenty-five years earlier, when a strange man raped me, at about the same time of the morning.

To assuage my fears of her possible demise while traveling, I purchased a car for her. It was a dark blue 1991

Toyota Camry, complete with power steering and power windows. She liked the color blue. Her previous two cars were that color. I even paid the insurance on the car until 1994 when I finally moved out of the house.

My mother used this car until she stopped driving completely in 2006, at the age of eighty-two. The odometer had clocked a mere 65,000 miles, averaging out to approximately 4,300 miles per year, proving just how little she drove.

Another way she encouraged me to remain living with her was that she allowed me to build a darkroom in her garage. From most people's perspectives, this would appear odd. The majority of parents would have told their children, "No, this is my house. You are not modifying it. After all, you will not be here forever."

Instead, my mother gave me carte blanche to build a fully functioning darkroom, taking out several feet of her garage that could have been used for additional parking or storage. Looking back on it, this was a clear indication she never intended for me to leave.

Although I lived under her roof, she pretty much stayed out of my business. In fact, in certain respects, she treated me more like her spouse than her daughter. The minute I strolled in the door from work, she started chattering, telling me all about her day. Often, I had worked long and hard that day and simply wanted to relax, but as I toddled through the door, before I could get my coat off or put down my purse, she would launch straight in to asking me if I knew about such and such, or she would begin to inform me of her day's events.

Usually, I snapped at her, "Can't I get settled, before you have to tell me about everything?" Sometimes, I even lamented, "I'm not your husband! Why do you have to tell me everything, the minute I walk through the door?" As the years passed, this particularly annoying habit of hers was fodder for our increasing arguments.

Whenever I yelled at her, she immediately gave me the cold shoulder. She was an expert at making me feel guilty. When I chastised her for treating me like a husband, she would stop talking to me for days. Not only would she cease speaking, she would hang her head, slumping over as if I had struck her through the heart with a knife.

She could stay in this martyred stance for days, until it became unbearable for me. I always gave in and apologized to keep the peace. Only after I said I was sorry first, did she make up with me. She never initiated the reconciliation.

I tried to hold out when I had a disagreement with my mother, to allow her the opportunity to say she was sorry. Although I was wrong some of the time and owed her an apology, I was not in the wrong every time. With each battle and every time I gave in, my self-esteem sunk lower, and I became surer of one thing; my mother did not care about me as much as I had hoped or wanted. It was becoming more and more clear to me that, despite my hopes otherwise, my mother did not demonstrate that I was of much value.

I was not the only one in our family who noticed her actions appeared to devalue my siblings and me, that is, all my siblings with the exception of Terry, the oldest. It had always been obvious to the rest of us that my mother showed favoritism when it came to her first-born. She staunchly denied the allegation whenever it came up, but the facts proved otherwise.

As an adult, my little brother Paul questioned my mother's motives for giving Terry her own bedroom when we were growing up. And sometimes, when we moved into a new house, my mother gave Terry the master bedroom. So, not only did she get her own room, she got the largest one in the house. She was also given her own phone and her own car, a yellow Toyota Corolla, when she graduated high school. These were things the rest of us were never afforded.

My younger brother asked my mother why Terry had always had her own bedroom, when the remainder of the siblings barely fit into our tiny rooms. Some of us, like my two youngest sisters, Jeanne and Patty, did not even have a room most of the time. They slept on the couch in the living room. My parents converted the dining room into a makeshift bedroom, which was used by either Tommy and Paul or Mary and me.

What was even more contentious was the fact that Terry had a size full bed. Tommy, Paul, Mary, and I all had twin beds. Since Terry had a larger bed, it would have made sense that my mother could have at least allowed one of my little sisters to sleep in Terry's room, but this never happened.

When Paul asked my mother why there was such an imbalance with our sleeping arrangements, she could not provide an answer. I do not know if he was satisfied. I only know he questioned the situation.

He was not the only one who had noticed a discrepancy in our household room assignments. The rest of us had discussed this very subject among ourselves. To me, it was further validation my mother felt Terry was more worthy of her affection than the rest of us.

Mary also took issue with my mother's noticeable bias towards Terry. When we were growing up, Mary regularly fought with Mother about this very subject. The rest of us kept quiet until we were adults, but not Mary. She not only questioned the sleeping arrangements, she was upset over other things. For instance, my oldest sister was given several childhood birthday parties by my mother, but none of the rest of us ever were, except for Mary, who only got a party of her own because she threw a fit after my mother turned her down when she asked for one. Mary demanded to know why Terry was the only one who got parties. After many hours of arguing, my mother finally conceded, permitting Mary a similar bash.

Almost every time Terry had an event or program that was at the same time as one of the other siblings', my mother usually chose to go to Terry's. Since Mary is four years younger than Terry, when Mary graduated from eighth grade, Terry was having her high school graduation. As fate would have it, Mary's graduation ceremony fell on the exact same day as Terry's. Mother chose to go to Terry's graduation not Mary's.

Four years later, Mary was the valedictorian of her class and she anticipated the likely outcome since Terry was also graduating from college. It initially appeared that my mother was again going to miss Mary's graduation. Mary was furious. "I'm valedictorian," she ranted. "What does it take for you to acknowledge me? You always attend Terry's functions. It is not fair!"

My mother's only explanation was, "Terry is the oldest. Besides, she is graduating from college. She is the first to do this. When you get to college, I'll attend your ceremony."

Mary was, understandably, not happy with my mother's decision, until my mother conceded and attended Mary's ceremony since Terry's graduation was not at the same time.

But the day of Mary's wedding gave, in my view, the best example of my mother's preferential treatment of Terry. My mother behaved repugnantly that day. A few short hours before the ceremony, she interrupted Mary's preparations to say, "You know, Mary, Terry is hurt because you did not ask her to be in the wedding party. I think you should have asked her."

Mary felt it was wrong of my mother to tell her who to include in her own wedding. Besides, if Terry was upset, she could have spoken to Mary herself. No matter what Terry's real feelings were, my oldest sister never indicated to Mary that she was upset about being excluded.

Furthermore, Mary did not ask every one of her sisters to be in the wedding party. Not only did she exclude Terry, she also excluded my youngest sister Patty. But my mother wasn't concerned about Patty's feelings.

Her timing was terrible. Waiting to speak with Mary about it until her wedding day showed just how selfish she could be. Mary felt that her mother was attempting to ruin her wedding day. My mother knew damn well there was no way Terry could be included at the last minute, but she brought it up anyway. The usual battle ensued. In the end, my mother cruelly accomplished her mission—she upset Mary and put a damper on her special day.

While most families naturally take many pictures of their firstborn and show a decline in the number of photos taken of subsequent children once the novelty wears off, in our family, this was not the case. There are numerous photographs of Terry, but practically none of the rest of us. There is no slow decline of pictures with each birth; it just halts abruptly after the oldest. In fact, the rest of us are lucky if we can find one single baby picture, which made it impossible to provide them, when requested, for school projects and such.

When we asked my mother why there was such a discrepancy, she merely replied, "We did not have any money to take pictures of you."

She could not explain why they had money for the oldest, though. The fact is, my parents never had much money, even when Terry was born. Actually, my mother quit working when she married my dad and only began working again after my youngest sister was born. So their only source of income before that time was from my dad, who never made much because he jumped from job to job.

My mother's own words corroborate their financial hardship when Terry was the only one running around. My parents owned a bakery in Muenster, Texas, when Terry was a baby. My mother always said, "We learned pretty quickly you could not make any money in the bakery business, in a small town. People baked their own bread. Since everyone knew us, they expected cheaper goods or free stuff."

Still, we did not believe my parents had money for pictures of Terry but not for the rest of us. After all, it did not make sense that the money just dried up after the first child. Maybe this would be the case after three or four children, but certainly not after only one child.

My mother once said to me, "The oldest holds a special place in one's heart. You do not understand because you do not have children of your own. But, if you did, you'd understand."

This confirmed that my mother loved Terry more than the rest of us. Not only that, but she seemed to take pride in rubbing in my face the fact that I did not have any children of my own (a fact she seemed eager to perpetuate by doing her damned best to keep me from marrying).

The result was that even though my mother loved Terry more, her wanting us to love Terry as much as she did caused the opposite effect. We grew to resent Terry for the privileges she was given. Instead of making Terry loved by all, she alienated Terry from us. My mother not only destroyed our own worth, but she destroyed the child she loved the most. She did a disservice to both Terry and us.

In the end, although Terry was favored as a child, it affected her detrimentally. I know it was not Terry's fault she was favored. The responsibility rested solely with my mother.

Chapter 21

Rumblings

When we were in our teens and started going out, we never had curfews. We could come home at any hour of the night without reprimand. As a teenager, I thought this was great. In reality though, parents give their children curfews so they will not have to spend all night worrying and waiting for their children to return home. It is precisely because parents care about their children that they find it beneficial to enforce curfews. Without them, they worry.

My dad did wait up for us, on occasion. Sometimes, when I came home at four in the morning, my dad was sitting within view of the front door, smoking his cigarette and drinking a beer. He never said a word but went to bed shortly after the last one of us arrived home. It was obvious to me that he was somewhat concerned about us, despite the no-curfew policy in our household.

My mother, on the other hand, never waited up. If she was worried about us, her actions did not dictate it, as she always went to bed, sleeping soundly while we were out on the town. Maybe this was because she knew my dad was already up, but she was aware that he drank heavily, and if something unfortunate had happened to one of us, he may not have been conscious enough to alert her to a problem.

Besides not having curfews, we never had a set bedtime at any time in our childhood. All I know is, my mother used to say, "You know when to go to bed; your punishment will be when you have to get up in the morning."

Most nights we were in bed by ten p.m., but we could stay up as late as we wanted. So sometimes, we went to bed much later.

Since my parents did not have much, our family typically lived in a small house with only one bathroom. It must have helped my mother tremendously for us to be able to stay up so late, because we could take our baths then. Maybe that is why she never set a bedtime. But she deferred the parenting role to us by telling us we knew when to go to bed. Again, at the time, I did not complain. Why should I? How was I to know any better? I was only a kid.

In my teens, I worked as a waitress for a local Mexican-food restaurant. After work, many of the employees went out on the town, playing foosball or pool, eating pizza, and drinking. One day there was a new waitress working with me, who had transferred from another store. Her name was Drusilla, or Drusy for short. She was very personable and quickly joined our group that partied after hours. Drusy and I hit it off immediately, and within weeks, she and I became very close friends, forming a friendship that has lasted for over thirty years.

Within the course of our barhopping, we became groupies of a local pop band. We spent many nights going to see this band in bars. We also frittered our time away on numerous occasions, driving around town, laughing and giggling in the car and commenting on guys who came across our path.

I soon discovered my father was getting unnerved by the amount of time I was spending with Drusilla. He noticed I was not dating men, but was instead wasting an inordinate amount of time with a girl. It bothered him. I later learned from my mother that he voiced his opinions to her, thinking I might be a lesbian, which was a grave sin to him.

I found out about his negative feelings towards my best friend when I asked my mother why my father was so rude to Drusy. Whenever Drusy came over to the house, she hugged and kissed him, but he would turn his head, making an awful frown and would slap his hand back and forth through the air, as if instructing her to get away from him. Since he never did this with anyone else, I knew something was up.

Drusy came from a family who normally greeted each other with a kiss and hug, a quality I found endearing, especially since true affection was so lacking in our family. I remember my dad giving kisses when we were very small, but I do not even recall my mother ever hugging and kissing us.

My mother actually detested little kids kissing her on the lips. After one of her grandkids tried to kiss her, she told me, "I can't stand that slobber coming out of their mouths. I don't want to be kissed on the lips." It was as if she was afraid she would get cooties or something.

It was rare that my parents ever showed true affection in front of us. Even with this being the case, my mother was pregnant more than a half dozen times. Therefore, I know they had some kind of chemistry.

After my dad died, my mother could have easily remarried. She is a beauty and looks much younger than her age. She was only fifty-seven years old when my dad died in 1981. However, on many occasions, when I expressed my wish that she get out and date, she replied, "I had my man, I don't want another."

I am not sure what she meant by this. I know she had a hard life with my father. He was a domineering, loud, and brash man, an alcoholic who jumped from job to job. Whenever he was drunk, he became more obnoxious. Considering all of these factors, it surely must have been difficult for her. Maybe this was the cause for her comment.

Although it made me angry that my father might think I was a lesbian, at least he was concerned that I was not dating men, as other females my age commonly might have done. However, my mother just shrugged it off. She told my dad that Drusy was only a friend and that his worries were unfounded.

She was glad I was not interested in men. She was always dissuading me from dating. She said to me, incredulously, when one of my brothers or sisters had girlfriend, boyfriend, or marriage problems, "And YOU want to get married!"

I always felt, she did not want me to find a man to love me, and as I aged we had more and more arguments over this very issue, but she always denied the accusation, though I was not the only one who witnessed her obvious intentions to the contrary.

In the fall of 1993, I invited my mother to go to Germany with two of my good friends and me. We needed a fourth person in our group, and I thought that since she was of German descent and had always expressed an interest in traveling to Germany, she would love to make the trip with us. My friends liked her and were happy she could accompany us.

The trip was a bargain for the time. We were able to secure our tickets from a travel agency who had a special deal with one of the local radio stations in Dallas. The trips offered were at substantially low prices. Because the savings were so great, the spaces available for each of these excursions filled quickly. There was a catch: you had to leave within several weeks of booking the tour. Luckily, all four of us had the ability to take time off at a moment's notice to travel to Germany.

Our trip included round-trip airfare from Dallas to Germany, room and board at mid-priced hotels, continental breakfast every morning, three dinners, and a tour of Germany and Switzerland, complete with tour bus and sightseeing guide for the entire week of our journey.

On our first morning in Germany, she began to show her insecurities towards my having an outside life that did not include her. As we were eating breakfast with the rest of the tour group, she made it a point to embarrass me. Specifically, she told the people in our group that I did not want her to travel with me. She mentioned this towards the end of the meal, after everyone at our table had grown fond of her.

My mother was charming and fooled the other travelers with her charisma. No one was aware of how unkind or neglectful she could be, or of the resulting events that happened in my life. She came across as a benevolent, older woman. She was just a few months shy of seventy at the time.

It did not matter that I had not said anything of the sort or that I did not feel the way she claimed. After all, I had invited her on the trip and would not have done so if I did not want her to travel with me. Her words shocked me.

I could sense the stare from each of the other tourists at the table. I quickly tried to dissolve the message, saying, "I never said that!" but the damage was done.

Of course, she did not reply to my rebuttal. She just sat there. How could she reply? She fully knew it was a lie. Looking back on it, I realized I was in the middle of a conversation with a man when she made her proclamation. I surmise she must have felt threatened.

Shortly afterward, something else happened on that trip that solidified my awareness of her true nature and feelings on my involvement with a man. As we began touring the countryside, people quickly filled each of the seats. Since each of the seats accommodated two people, my two friends usually sat together in one seat, while my mother and I occupied another.

Most people had two or four people in their party, but there were a few people traveling alone, which meant that if you were one of the last parties to board the bus, there was a chance you had to split up because of a lack of empty two-man seats.

On our second day of touring, since my mother was moving slower than most of the other passengers, we were the last people to board the bus. As a result, there were only spaces for singles left; my mother and I would have to sit apart on this leg of the journey.

My two friends had already boarded, and as I stepped on the bus, one of them mouthed to me, "Cindy, sit over there with that guy. We saved that seat for you!"

They were referring to a young, handsome man about my age who was traveling alone. This was their attempt to set me up with a possible date, but my mother also saw the comment and quickly marched over to that man's chair and sat next to him. I had no other choice but to sit in the only other space on the bus, next to a middle-aged woman.

As we reached the first stop on our tour, one of my two friends commented to my mother, "Hey, what's the deal? Why are you sitting next to that young, cute guy? Why don't you give that seat to Cindy, because she is closer to his age?"

My mother completely ignored her and continued to sit with the man each time we boarded the bus.

Later, after my mother had retired for the evening, I went to my friends' room for a visit. When I was alone with them, they informed me that they were indignant about my mother's actions.

Angrily, they said, "Your mother is deliberately trying to keep you from meeting a man. It is obvious to us. We are very upset with her."

When I heard this, I realized I had been correct in my assumption that she never wanted me to marry. Here was outside proof; I hadn't been imagining this.

My mother had flirted with the young man on the bus. It was as if she was competing with me for his attentions. The fact that she would do this made me even more disappointed with her. After all, why would she not want me to enjoy the company of a young man? I do not know her true reasons for such bad behavior. However, it seemed to me that she was afraid I would marry and leave her. She had grown too dependent on me since my dad's death.

When we got home, she continued the flirtation, much to my chagrin. The young man from the bus had videotaped the tour through Germany. Shortly after our return, he called, saying he had made an extra copy of the videotape and wanted to give it to me to share with my mother as a remembrance of the trip. I was touched and decided to have him over for dinner, along with my two friends who had taken the trip with us.

I asked my mother if I could have some privacy with my friends, but my simple request made her mad. She launched into guilt-provoking treatment of me, pouted, and didn't talk for days. I finally acquiesced rather than face her wrath, but I paid the price for surrendering. Even though I included her, she invariably, purposefully embarrassed me in front of my friends.

On the night of the dinner, my mother continued to flirt with my male friend, just as she had done in Germany. Her intention was unmistakable. She dressed as if she were going on a date, wearing a bright red sweater to accent her looks. She thanked him profusely for the videotape, as if it was hers alone, and the entire night, she kept guiding his attention away from me. By the end of the night, I was completely fed up. As he and my friends were leaving, I arose to hug and kiss them goodnight. I was appalled when my mother shot up to hug and kiss them, effectively crowding me out. She followed them out the door, just as I was hoping to steal a few minutes alone with them.

The anger welled in me at last, and I snapped at her, "Mother, do you mind? These are MY friends!"

With this admonishment, she finally retreated into the house, but the damage was done. The fact that I yelled at my mother in front of my friends made me look bad anyway.

Of course, we ended up having a huge argument after this encounter. It occurred several days later because she would not talk to me after I chastised her that night. I was the one who had to apologize. I do not know if she really thought she was not acting inappropriately or if she was just in denial about the whole affair. I only knew it would be a cold day in hell before she would ever initiate a ceasefire with me.

Even years later, after she moved in with me, she continued her efforts of humiliating me in front of my friends. I was more forceful and had grown wiser by the time she began living with me, and I decided her actions were not going to thwart me any longer. Therefore, whenever I had a dinner party, I arranged for her to spend time with one of my other siblings. Usually, she would spend the night at Mary's house, because my sister only lived a little over a mile from us.

This arrangement worked beautifully for the most part. Extracting my mother from the premises assured me that I would be able to enjoy myself fully, without her attempts to spoil the evening distracting me. But my mother was stubborn and, on one occasion, was successful in her spiteful behavior despite my best-laid plans.

I was having a Christmas dinner party for several of my closest friends. It had become an annual tradition with me. As usual, I had arranged for my mother to spend the night elsewhere. Mary gladly took her in for the evening. There were six of us at the dinner table: my best friend, two female friends I knew from work, one male friend who also worked with me, a male artist friend of mine, and myself.

As we were delving into our desert, the front door suddenly opened. It was my mother. She made my sister bring her back home, because she was ready to go to sleep and said she had to sleep in her own bed.

My sister argued with her when she made the request but ended up complying instead of fighting with her, further proof my mother was a stubborn, old bird. As it turned out, I was not the only person who lost battles with her.

As she walked in the door, she saw my shocked face and responded with, "I wanted to sleep in my own bed, so Mary brought me home."

My friends did not know about my ulterior motives to get her out of the house. One of them, as a courtesy, asked her to join us. It didn't matter anymore that she said she was ready to go to bed when she walked into the house; she pulled up a chair and began to tear into the cheesecake I had served.

The whole atmosphere of the evening changed. Before she arrived, we were laughing and giggling. After she joined us, everyone was subdued out of respect for my mother.

I was angry, and my mother, sensing my disapproval, suddenly announced to the group, "Cindy kicked me out of the house. She does not want me here. So I guess I'd better go to bed."

I was too mortified to respond. Within moments, she extricated herself from the table and went off to bed, leaving me to endure the looks from my close friends. She had managed to spoil the evening after all. Of course, she darn well knew it.

What made me even more displeased with her was the fact that we had already discussed such behavior before. We had a fight over a similar situation while we were in Germany, when my mother had announced I didn't want her there. Despite our resulting fight, she was adamant about repeating the pattern. Tonight's actions proved to me just how cruel she could be, as she was aware how I would feel about such an admonition in front of my friends.

I can only guess she acted this way that evening because she knew I had two male friends coming to the party. She could not risk my involvement with one of them. She did not want me to marry. So she deliberately left Mary's to come upset things for me.

When I asked her to move in with me, she replied, "You're not going to get married are you? Don't run off with someone or I won't have a place to stay!"

This statement said it all; she was thinking only of herself.

At the time, I quickly reprimanded her for her comment, exclaiming, "Now wait a minute! I don't want you moving in with me if you think I won't get married."

Since she really wanted to move in with me, she did not put up a fight at the time. Instead, she coolly responded as if she never even made the remark, "Oh no. I want you to get married." However, no matter what words she spoke to the contrary, her actions would continue to prove otherwise.

Chapter 22

Damaged Love: Overlooking the Flaws

I can only speculate why my mother would want to keep me from marrying. It was the same reason she did not encourage me to move out of her house. I am assuming it was because she needed me, emotionally, to fill the void left in her heart when my dad died.

I was doing a fairly decent job of filling that void. I took her on annual driving trips across the country and invited her to large gatherings at the house. My mother reveled and participated in these affairs.

It was impossible not to invite her, because it was her house and she felt entitled to attend. If I suggested she go elsewhere for the day, she was insulted. She could have easily gone to visit one of her other six children, as they all lived in the Dallas–Fort Worth area. Instead, she made a fuss. Since she was such an expert at making me feel guilty, I always invited her.

My mother always told me how much she loved my father. She said it was why she waited years to marry him. She had gone against her parents' wishes to date him and finally followed him across the country when he moved to California. During her marriage, she stayed true to her marriage vows: through sickness and health, for richer and poorer. I suppose it was because she loved him that she overlooked his many faults, including the fact he was fondling his own children. I am positive she colluded with him in this.

I know she knew about it because she once stated to me that she thought, "Daddy had done something to . . . "

At the time, I questioned her and asked, "What do you mean?"

I fully knew what she meant, but I had to hear it from her mouth. I was shocked that she could have known all along what my father was doing and yet did nothing to stop it.

She said, "You know, messed with her."

There was no mistake. "Messed with" was the same phrase she had used when she told me that her grandfather had touched her sexually. If she suspected my father had done something sexually to one of her other daughters, she must have known he was capable of it and could have done it to me.

This conversation was a stunning revelation that my mother may not have been as innocent of my father's actions as I thought.

Another irony was that, although my mother was a dedicated Catholic and did not believe in divorce, she told me she once served divorce papers to my dad when I was just about four or five years old. She said my dad was unemployed and he decided to move to Austin, a city about two hundred miles south of Dallas, to find work.

He left her alone with six kids and one on the way, without any money. He was gone for weeks. She was fed up with his shenanigans and tried to get him to come home because the bills were piling up. She just knew he was out having a good time while she was stuck taking care of toddlers and small children, so my mother decided to divorce my dad and served him papers. It did the trick; my dad came home and got a job.

Her view of sex also seemed to be very warped. She acted as if it was bad. She was particularly offended when TV shows aired sex scenes. "I don't want to watch that filth," would be her comment. Anytime a television program aired a sex scene, she snubbed her nose, griped, and insisted we turn the channel—even when we were adults.

This annoyed me because I thought she was being duplicitous. For one thing, she religiously watched soap operas and never seemed offended by the bed hopping and many divorces portrayed in those shows.

As I grew older, I became more irritated with her view of sex. After all, she did have sex often enough to have seven children. How bad could it have been?

I know my mother and father once had a healthy sex life, because I heard them having sex when I was about ten years old. At the time, my bedroom was right next to my parents' room. I had awoken in the middle of the night to strange sounds coming from their room. I first thought my father was hurting my mother, but soon realized my mother liked whatever he was doing; I could tell from the comments she made. I was scared at the time and covered my ears, but I could hear them anyway. I never told anyone about this private moment my parents' shared. However, whenever my mother made a remark about sex being bad, I knew from what I had heard that she liked it once upon a time.

My mother always had someone to look after her, until I up and left when I was thirty-seven. But in the summer of 2000, I temporarily moved back in with my mother. By then she had been living by herself for about seven years. While living there, I noticed a decline in her state of affairs. She was not eating properly and was having a hard time making ends meet.

As I had purchased some property and begun construction of a new home, I decided it would be beneficial for my mother, if she were to move in with me, as it was obvious she was getting too old to care for herself. At the time, she was seventy-seven.

I modeled and built my home with her in mind, choosing an open floor plan and expanding the bathroom so she could move about easily, should a walker or wheelchair ever confine her. I invited her to live with me when my house was finished. However, she was reluctant to leave her home where she had lived for almost thirty years.

My new home was completed in 2001, and I moved out of her house once again. Afterwards, I continued to encourage my mother to consider moving over to my place. She would often spend time at my house and seemed to enjoy it tremendously. It took about a year of coaxing from all of her children to get my mother to agree to move in with me. In the fall of 2002, she relocated permanently to my address and put her house on the market.

Chapter 23

Dirty Onion Sack

Shortly after my mother moved in with me, I was going through some of her old papers and discovered the shock of my life. She was a pack rat and had boxes of old checks and tax returns that went all the way back to the 1950s. Since I did not want this excess garbage over at my house, I decided to shred the works. I asked her permission to discard these items.

She said, "I don't want them. Go ahead and throw them out."

While I was sorting through these documents, I found an old onion sack, filled with miscellaneous papers and photo negatives. It had been stored in the garage at her house. While cleaning out her garage in preparation for her move, my older brother had come across the sack. Noticing some important documents inside, he decided to give it to my mother. He told her to go through the bag and destroy anything that was no longer useful.

One day I told my mother I was going to tackle the onion sack, and she said, "Great, better you than me."

With this permission, I started pulling the items from the sack, one by one. Here I discovered numerous truths about my parents. Some of the interesting items I found in this sack included: an affidavit and warrant of search and seizure—presented to my dad when he owned his own bakery in Muenster, Texas—for unlawful storage of liquor; my parents wedding invitation; a handwritten letter from my maternal grandparents to my parents, offering them best wishes on the birth of my oldest sister; a list of handwritten expenses for the household, dated 1963; the airline ticket stubs used by my parents when they flew from California to Texas on April 12, 1952, to surprise my maternal grandparents with a visit; a typewritten sheet entitled "Suggested Regulations for Girls Attending USO Socials" that was given to my mother when she attended USO dances during World War II; a letter from the USO outlining an award to be presented to my mother for meritorious service, dated June 24, 1944; and partial remnants of handwritten letters from twelve-year-old Terry to my mother, who was in the hospital having a hysterectomy.

It was a treasure trove of information, previously hidden in plain sight in the garage. No one would have ever thought that this dirty, ugly, flimsy sack, once used to hold onions, could yield so much; yet the contents proved ever so enlightening.

It was both fun and weird going through the sack, discovering new information. It was fun because I could piece together a snapshot of different points in time of my parents' lives. It was strange because no one ever knew these things existed—not even my mother. She thought they were long gone.

Uncovering item after item, I asked my mother, who was nonchalantly watching television the entire time I rummaged through the sack, about each. She obligingly shared the stories that went along with each item. That is, until I unearthed one startling letter.

I had pulled out a letter from my father addressed to a woman whose name was unfamiliar to anyone in our family, except my mother, as I found out. I read the letter and was shocked to discover that my dad had asked for a divorce from this woman. From the contents of the letter, it was apparent he had been trying to get a response from her for some time.

I couldn't believe he was divorced. My mother would never have married a man who was divorced. It was against everything she had taught us. As a matter of fact, she had often told us she would never have married my Protestant dad if he hadn't converted to Catholicism. But divorce was a definite no-no in the Catholic faith back then, and my mother professed that she was devout Catholic; yet she married a divorced man.

Still more alarming was the fact that she managed to keep the fact that my father was previously married a secret from my siblings and me, until I uncovered the letter at the age of forty-five. That was a long time to keep something so important concealed. I suspect my parents had hoped to take this astounding information with them to the grave; however, although my father was able to accomplish this feat, my mother was on the chopping block.

When I inquired about the letter, she suddenly froze and said rather quickly, "Give me that letter!"

That my father had even kept the letter visibly shook her.

She said, "I did not know your Daddy had this letter."

"Why did you not tell us about this?" I asked.

"It wasn't your business," she responded, but I kept pressing her for answers; it was time for her to fess up.

My mother married my dad when she was twenty-seven. She was quite beautiful and, based on the many pictures she had of them, had attracted many suitors. However, when she met my dad, she fell deeply in love.

She used to tell us how her parents never liked my father. When he decided to move to California, I am sure they were happy. But she could not live without him and soon followed him to the West Coast from Texas, some three years prior to their marriage.

This fact had always fascinated me, for the mother I knew was not independent—relying first on my father and then me when he had died—though this proved she once had been very self-sufficient.

She never said much about living in Los Angeles, other than that she worked at the May company. I did know that both my parents moved to the San Francisco area, though neither of them ever discussed why or how they moved to San Francisco.

Since ours was a family where our parents taught us to keep everything to ourselves, none of us had really questioned how they ended up in Northern California.

However, it wasn't until February 3, 1951, that my dad finally wed my mother in El Cerrito, California. He was thirty-one years old. My mother had been dating him for approximately four years.

It is funny how the truth always comes out, despite our best attempts to hide it. Caught burying the truth, my mother explained the letter to me. When she met and began dating my dad, at the age of twenty-three, he was already married, though he had told her the marriage was over. Even though he was not yet divorced, he wanted a divorce. In addition, my dad and his future ex-wife had not lived together for quite some time.

My mother said she did not actually know much about his ex-wife. She only knew that my father now loved her and wanted a divorce from his wife. But it took years for the divorce to be finalized, which was the real reason my parents waited so many years to get hitched.

Things were making more sense to me now. This explained my grandparents' immense dislike of my father. They were devout Catholics, and for my mother to be interested in a married man was against their religion.

I always thought it was odd that my mother and father waited four long years to get married. After all, back in 1951 my mother would have been considered an old maid at the age of twenty-seven.

My mother was obviously agitated about the whole conversation, so I did not push for more information.

I then found a bank booklet, outlining deposits and withdrawals from 1948 to 1951, from a joint account in both my mother and father's names. What was strange about this was that the account was used for several years before my parents ever got married.

I asked my mother why they had an account together, but she grabbed the booklet quickly from me, answered vaguely, and refused to elaborate. I have never seen it or the letter from my dad to his first wife since that day.

I knew there was something more to this story. I wondered if they had lived together, which would have been a logical explanation for why the bank issued the account under one address only.

My mother had always made derogatory comments about others who lived together. She thought it was a sin.

"Did you live with Daddy?" I asked.

"No, of course not! We only had an account together."

This reply still did not satisfy me, but I knew I had better leave it alone. She was upset, and I was not in the mood to deal with an argument.

Several years later, I began working on our family tree. As I was researching my dad's name, I found four legal notices in a Reno, Nevada, newspaper. These were notices given as a prerequisite for a divorce. I found them in the 1950 September and October editions of the *Reno Gazette*. The notices listed my dad as the plaintiff and his ex-wife as the defendant.

From the notices, I gathered that my dad was attempting to obtain a divorce on the grounds that they had not cohabitated in more than three years. Each notice summoned my dad's ex-wife to contest the divorce within a certain number of days. Here was more proof that my dad was married. I had to find out more, so I showed my mother the notices. Even though my mother had previously wanted to keep this part of her life a secret, she knew I would not rest until I had more answers.

"Look at this, Mother," I exclaimed as I presented them to her.

With a frown on her face, she told me bluntly that she did not know about the notices, but when she saw the dates, a familiarity came across her face, as if a light bulb suddenly turned on.

She said, "So that's what he was doing in Reno."

"What do you mean? Didn't you know he was getting a divorce?" I asked.

"No. I thought he went to gamble and drink. I was mad at him because he was gone for so long, and he left me to pay the bills. He never told me about doing any of this."

My ears pricked up when she mentioned paying the bills. If they were not living together, why would she be paying the bills?

In the end, I decided against pursuing the subject. We had already gone over this, and I knew she would be very defensive. I did begin to wonder how much she really knew about my father before she married him. It was plain to see that she hadn't discussed his divorce with him.

My mother loved to watch *Judge Judy* on television and comment on some of the cases. Whenever Judge Judy chastised a woman for getting involved with a man she barely knew, or who obviously hid things from her, my mother emphatically added: "Those stupid women! Don't they know men cannot be trusted? Women fall head over heels in love with someone they do not even know. They should have known better!"

I found it absurd that my mother found fault with these women on television when, in my opinion, she had been in the same boat.

So now the complete picture had come into focus. My mother had followed my dad to Los Angeles in 1948. He tried to get a divorce from his ex-wife, but she was not responding. In the fall of 1950, he decided to go to Reno, Nevada, to obtain a divorce, unbeknownst to my mother. Logically, because he was absent for over a month, he must have lost his job in Los Angeles. Then when my father went looking for a new job, he must have found employment in Northern California. That is probably why my parents moved to the San Francisco area. They married in El Cerrito, California, a little over three months after the last notice posted in Reno. They must have married as soon as the divorce was final.

I knew my father kept secrets. For instance, my dad could speak German fluently, though no one in my immediate family was aware of this fact until after he died. All through our lives, he would throw out short German phrases, but we just assumed he only knew those few phrases. It was not until after he passed that we learned the truth from his younger brother.

My father rarely spoke of his feelings or his childhood. The fact that he did not tell us he could speak fluent German was a testament to this trait. In fact, we were never encouraged to ask questions from either parent. Because my father was so closed off, and because we also were emotionally unattached, we failed to see reality. How he could keep such a secret from his family defies logic.

So when I found that letter, exposing a surreptitious event in my father's life, it did not surprise me that he had kept the information hushed. I simply had not anticipated that my mother was keeping secrets also. That onion sack established that my father had scandalous skeletons in the closet, things he kept from us but not from my mother. She had managed to keep her mouth closed about a vital piece of information—a secret so profound that it could have ultimately destroyed everything she had taught us. I wondered what else she had kept from us, since she had managed to keep this divorce, which went against her own belief system, a secret.

I wondered if I would be able to respect her, knowing this hypocrisy. It was painfully evident to me that my mother had a double standard. She sermonized that it was bad to marry someone who had been previously married, yet she had done this very thing. Additionally, my mother had always decried that it was a sin to live with a man before marriage, but it was apparent from the information I found in the garage and her subsequent comments regarding paying the bills for the household from their joint banking account that they may very well have been living together. Perhaps not, but since she could not give me a reasonable explanation for why they had such an account together, I was skeptical. Was everything she had preached against her whole life a lie? If it was not, she was not very good at convincing me otherwise.

All this only further emphasized to me that I was angry with my mother. I was angry for her actions when I was nine. A strange man raped me, a doctor invaded my body, and my own father fondled me in the most inappropriate way. She never protected me, either from them or from stalking perverts. After all this time, I blamed her. It was because of those events and her actions toward me on the day of my rape, that I was questioning her parental skills. The rape simply started an unstoppable chain of terrible occurrences.

I wondered how could she let that doctor touch me without at least comforting me first, how could she let my father fondle me, and why did she not protect me. But most of all, I wondered how she could allow my sister and me to venture out into the darkness, at about four in the morning, by ourselves.

Mary and I were too young and innocent to imagine a dangerous environment outside our home. That was our parents' job. I needed nurturing care from my mother, but I was rudely disappointed. It was surprising really that someone had not kidnapped us sooner.

Later, my mother would tell me that "times were different in the 1960s." This was probably her way of justifying to herself the atrocity of letting her babies go out into a wicked world without any supervision. I did not believe her when she told me times were different, not in a big city like Dallas.

Over time, this anger and distress I felt towards her, regarding her lack of care in my youth, grew to such a degree that I felt that I was at war with her. I realized that until I learned to release my hold on the war, it would affect me dramatically. It took listening to my instincts to find the road to healing.

Part Four

Changing My Future

Chapter 24

Moving Forward

The terrible events that had happened during my childhood shoved me into a deep depression, which lasted for many years. Most people did not know just how depressed I was most of my life. Hiding this from them, I put on a show of joviality and happiness. The actions of my mother, after my rape, programmed me to ignore any other feelings. I subconsciously thought it was bad to show others if I was upset, so I built up a facade to present to the outside world, but inside I was always in turmoil.

By the end of 2006, I was so depressed that I was seriously considering cutting my life short, and it took an enormous amount of effort to keep me from harming myself. I had always been taught that it was a sin to commit suicide, but it was more than that which kept me alive. It was a feeling, deep in my gut, that I should go on because things could get better. I weathered this pain, as I had so many other times in my life.

Another lesson taught to me, was that we are never given more than we can handle. I know this is true, because each time in my life when I thought I was at the breaking point, an angel was sent to rescue me. Mary was the first angel sent to console me when I was just an infant. And it happened again when Terry slipped into the bathroom and consoled me after my rape. It would also occur many other times in my life.

For instance, in 2005, I was very sick and had been off from work for over a year. Because of my condition, I was forced into seclusion. I woke one morning and was so isolated, alone, and depressed that I felt as if I was lower than the floor. As I struggled with my emotions, I unexpectedly received a call from a friend who I had not heard from in many, many months. She told me she just "got a feeling" that she must call me.

As we talked, she said, "I'm coming over right now to visit with you, as you are just too depressed. You need someone to talk to in person." She ended our conversation and was at my house within fifteen minutes. She stayed all afternoon, visiting with me and lifting my spirits.

During the afternoon, I remarked, "You are my angel."

She became emotional when I told her this. Then she relayed to me that she, too, was going through some tough times. Speaking to me had eased her pain. This knowledge helped me even more, as I became more aware of her pain instead of my own. By helping me, she received help herself. It showed me that it is better to allow others to be generous.

Because my friend listened to her inner voice and acted upon it, she benefitted from our afternoon together as much as I did. Not only do angels lift us up, but they can also indirectly set us on the path to healing and happiness. Although I had recognized that my friend was my angel, it turned out that I became her angel as well.

My best friend Drusilla became one of the most important angels in my life. Drusilla and I had many experiences spanning our thirty-year friendship. Our association with spirituality connected us more powerfully than if we were merely friends. It was for this reason that we liked to attend the local psychic fairs together, when we first became friends.

By the end of 2006, neither one of us had visited these fairs for almost twenty years. During one of our many conversations, she told me of her continuing interest in such matters and suggested we attend one of the upcoming fairs. I agreed to go with her. It would prove to be the most beneficial decision I ever made. Because of her suggestion, I changed my life's direction. It was totally unexpected!

The day of the psychic fair arrived. It was customary for the fair to begin at noon and last to around five thirty in the afternoon. About two dozen people would be giving the readings, incremented in fifteen-minute time slots per reader. The group included psychics, astrologers, palm readers, tarot card readers, tea-leaf readers, and the like.

Although the organization sponsoring the event only hosted experienced and results-proven readers, some were considered better than others by most attendees. Since this group had a larger following, many patrons arrived several hours early to be able to obtain a reading with one of these, perceived to be better, readers.

Drusy and I met early that morning at the hotel where the fair was held, so that we too would be assured of a reading with one of these popular readers. Since we had not been present at the event in so many years, we had to rely on the recommendations of others to influence our decisions of which readers to see that day.

The doors opened at eleven thirty, and the public soon began filling the various time slots with their favorite readers. Based on the comments we had heard, Drusilla and I decided on several readers each and began our day.

Although it would be ideal if everyone could book each reader consecutively, thereby finishing his or her readings sooner, this was not practical. For one thing, since there were so many people at the fair, the earlier time slots filled quickly. In addition, even though each reading was for fifteen minutes, sometimes the readers would inadvertently go over the time limit.

The organizers considered this fact for each reading request. If you booked more than one reading, they made sure you had ample time between readings to not miss your next slot. The fair also provided a number of round tables to accommodate patrons who were waiting or resting. Each table could seat about ten people.

The afternoon wore on, and when I finished my last scheduled reading, I seated myself at one of these tables to wait for Drusilla who was still with a reader. As I sat there, I contemplated whether I wanted to see any other readers. Curiously, even though the event was packed, there was no one else at my table, a most unusual situation.

Within a few moments of this observation, a woman sat down next to me. She was a slender woman of average height, with long, blond hair. Before I could speak, she began to expound the virtues of one of the readers. She said he was a shaman and a fantastic reader. She also said he gave weekly classes, which she attended, and that he had helped her tremendously. She quickly pointed him out to me, where he sat giving a reading across the room. His name was Charles Crooks.

I thanked her and turned away for a moment, to see if Drusy had finished her reading. When I turned back around to talk to the woman further, she had disappeared. I assumed she had left to have her own reading and did not think anything more of it.

Based on this woman's high regard of Mr. Crooks, I decided to have a reading with him. I went back to the assignment board and booked a fifteen-minute reading. As fate would have it, he had an opening almost immediately. Within minutes, I was seated before him at his table.

I had gone to the fair under the assumption the readers there would be able to ascertain my future. My past had been dismal, and I was looking for something better. I was hoping one of the readers could shed some light on the future and brighten the darkness I was experiencing.

However, I was actually disappointed with what the shaman said to me. Instead of telling me of wonderful things that would happen in the future, he only concentrated on my past.

He stated that I had a miserable past. Yeah, I did agree with that! But then he said it was not my fault. I was not so sure about that statement. He said I was carrying the blame around. He looked deeply into my eyes and told me I had good character. He also said he could help me, but it would take more than a fifteen-minute reading. Handing me one of his cards, he said, "It would be beneficial to you, if you came to see me privately."

Before I knew it, the reading was over. I remember getting up from the table thinking, "I will never see that man again!"

At the time, I thought most everything he had told me was true. However, I had wanted him to tell me about the future, as the others I had seen that day had attempted to do. It was not until months later that I would realize that Mr. Charles Crooks was the only person that day who provided me the answers I sought.

After I left the table, I hunted for my friend and found her standing in the foyer adjacent to the room. I told her adamantly, "Whatever you do, do not see Charles Crooks! He is only interested in getting you to see him privately!"

I left the fair that day dead set against ever seeing the shaman Charles Crooks again. I was wrong.

Chapter 25

Visiting a Shaman

Going to the psychic fair had somehow recharged me. I was still depressed, but instinctively, I felt things were going to get better. Because of this, I decided to take a more proactive approach to feeling better. Since I had been overweight just about my entire adult life, I decided to try something new to help me lose weight. That something was hypnosis.

On a whim, I called a hypnotherapist located only a few miles from my house. My first appointment with her was in early March. I enjoyed my sessions with her. She was a ray of hope, as she herself had been battling stage IV cancer for over six years. The doctors had given her only weeks to live many years prior. She attributed her continued life on this planet to her spirituality.

I felt an immediate connection to her, but the sessions were not helping me to lose weight. She did make me feel better simply by telling me I had a very good spirit. She declared she could see people's auras and told me that mine shone very brightly. I did not realize it at the time, but she also was an angel, instrumental in leading me to seek higher truths.

Because the hypnotherapy sessions were not working, I wondered if I would ever lose the weight that I so desperately wanted to drop. I could not explain it at the time, but within weeks of seeing the hypnotherapist, I began thinking, inexplicably, of the shaman I had met at the psychic fair in early February. For some reason, his name kept crossing my mind, even though I was so unimpressed with him at the fair. I wondered, *Could this man help me lose weight?*

One day I decided to look for his business card. I found it easily. I had many other business cards from readers I had seen at the fair, but his stood out. It was amazing that I had not thrown it away the day he gave it to me, since I was so resolutely against seeing him ever again. But here was his business card, and now I was contemplating reversing my decision.

His business card had a Web address listed on it which captivated me. It was www.healerofheartsandminds.com. It sounded so simple, yet profound. I decided to go to his Web site and read what was there.

As I opened the Web site, I was struck with admiration by the words on that first page. They simply read, "This site is dedicated to those before us who have labored in the Good Work. Their past efforts throughout the endless ages have set the stage for mankind's continual spiritual awakening. The terms Good Work and Continual Effort refers to the Spiritual Aspects of any effort carrying the attributes of; Love, Understanding, Compassion, Honesty, Honor, and Humility."

I felt an instantaneous connection. It was uncanny, but I felt I was home. I knew at that moment that I had to call Mr. Crooks to arrange a private meeting. Without hesitation, I picked up the phone and called him. He told me that he worked out of his home and gave me his address.

It was April 4, 2007. At the age of fifty, I drove over forty miles from my house to meet with Mr. Crooks for a private session. I knew nothing about this man, other than what was posted on his Web site and the fact that he held private sessions in his home.

I did not tell anyone—not even my best friend Drusilla—of my plans to see the man who referred to himself as a shaman, since I was sure it would raise eyebrows, and I was not prepared to deal with the probable onslaught of questions.

When I arrived at his home, he greeted me cordially and escorted me back to his meditation room, where he held his private sessions. The session took a little over two hours, and during that time, he chatted casually as he worked. I admit I was a little uneasy, as I was not altogether sure what he was doing, and it seemed strange at the time. He sat across the room from me. His hands appeared to be pulling something out of thin air. Later, he informed me that he had been "pulling stuff" out of me.

He explained to me that my weight was a form of protection. According to him, "It was impossible for you to be thin, given the hardships you endured."

He said that until I released my emotional baggage, I would continue to have weight issues. He explained that baggage included guilt for the terrible things that had occurred in my childhood.

He said, "You thought you were guilty because of the actions of your parents, especially your mother."

This is what he had been talking about on the day of the psychic fair! I now understood that this was the "stuff" that I had witnessed him pulling out of me.

I was amazed how he knew about the events that had happened when I was a child. He was not guessing, for he gave me details about my rapist that I had not shared with anyone. He also told me other things that he had no way of knowing. He reiterated once again, as he had on the day of the psychic fair, that I was not at fault for the events that had occurred in my life.

It would take months before I bought that line. It turned out he was right. However, cleaning up the scars left in my childhood was not that easy. I still had to release the emotions my mother never allowed me to express.

It was odd, but as he worked, I felt lighter and happier. The uneasiness I had experienced at first slipped away. Towards the end of the session, I even had an incredible vision.

When the session was over, I noted just how comfortable I felt with this man I barely knew. I discussed things of an extremely personal nature with him. I felt as if we could chat about any subject, no matter how disturbing. It was as if we had been friends for a long time. I never even felt compelled to address him formally. Since that day, I have always simply called him Charles. As he escorted me to the door, he wrapped his arms around me and gave me a warm, loving hug.

It was completely uncharacteristic of me to go to this man's house, knowing as little as I did about him. I had trust issues and was leery of strangers. This was especially true of men, given the circumstances that had happened to me when I was nine.

My best friend even remarked months later, when I finally told her about seeing him, "I cannot believe you would go to a strange man's house! Weren't you afraid?" I simply told her the truth: intuitively, I knew everything would be okay. I was not afraid, because I knew Mr. Charles Crooks was a good man and would not hurt me.

After that initial visit with him, my life would begin to change for the better. Moreover, the changes impressively appeared to be occurring very quickly, beginning the next day.

When I was a child, I had the most vivid dreams. The most significant thing I remember about my dreams was that they were always in color. The colors appeared more vibrant than in real life. Many times, I soared, flying high through the air. My dreams carried me over beautiful, aqua blue oceans and green rolling hills. I dreamed a lot in my younger years.

After my rape, however, there was a gradual decrease in my dreams. That is, if I did dream, upon waking I could not remember having dreamt. As the years passed, I appeared to dream less and less.

Before seeing Charles, I had been virtually dreamless for over ten years. However, the very night after seeing him, I began dreaming again. Not only did I begin to remember my dreams, the dreams took on the vivid, colorful hues that I had experienced as a child. Even though there had been a slow decline in my dreams over the years, the frequency of my dreams returned immediately to what it was in my pre-rape days.

More compelling evidence surfaced that indicated Charles had released something major the day I saw him. This had to do with my intuition. Although I had always had some sixth sense ability, after visiting with Charles, my talent grew stronger. I realized this the morning after my first session with Charles.

My dog Misha had passed several months earlier, in November 2006. Misha had liver dysfunction for several years. On November 28, 2006, her liver finally gave out, and I had to have her put to sleep.

I have another dog, Libby, who had grown up with Misha. Libby was very close to Misha and would follow her wherever she went. As I had other dogs that had died, I was cognizant of the fact that Libby would probably be grief-stricken over losing her beloved companion. Despite my concerns, Libby never really appeared to be terribly upset. Over the months, I got the impression that Misha's spirit was still hanging around the house.

I awoke the morning after seeing Charles to a heavy feeling on my chest. It was Misha. She was lying across my torso. Misha had weighed about forty-five pounds when she was living, and the feeling on my body was equivalent to this weight. Since it was too much for me to handle, I instructed Misha to jump off the bed. Immediately, I felt the weight lift. Then I heard her whimper and cry. I could tell she was sitting right next to the bed.

At this point, I sensed why she had been hanging around the house. She was worried about me. Realizing this, I encouraged her to leave, assuring her that I would be all right.

Just a few feet beyond my bed was the kennel where Misha had always slept when she was alive. I had never moved it out of the room. Within moments of relaying the wish for her to leave, I saw a bright light shoot up to the ceiling. Emanating from the spot right in front of her kennel, it resembled a shooting star.

I was amazed at what I had witnessed! Even though I had sensed Misha was in the house, before seeing Charles I never actually saw anything. Clearly, something had changed.

After that day, I never heard Misha in my house anymore, and Libby suddenly began the grieving process. I knew Misha had left the earth for good.

Chapter 26

Heaven-sent

A few short months after having that first private session with Charles, I recalled the circumstances that brought me to him. Specifically, I reflected about the words from the unknown woman at the psychic fair who had spoken so highly of Charles, thus prompting me to see him that day. I remembered she said he gave weekly classes and that she attended these classes regularly.

Since I wanted to facilitate an even faster progress, I began going to Charles's weekly classes on June 21, 2007. The first class drew me in completely. No matter how bad I felt or how tired I was before any class, I was always better and more energized after the class. From the moment I first began, I never missed one of his weekly classes.

As the months wore on, it was becoming evident my life had changed course. I was much happier and felt, for the first time in my life, that my life had purpose. I noticed it. Others noticed it as well.

Drusilla was the first to observe and comment on the significant change in my attitude and demeanor. She wanted to know what was going on. In response to her question, I finally revealed my secret. I told her of the private session I had with Mr. Crooks and the classes I was attending.

She was shocked that I could be seeing a man I had so adamantly disliked at the psychic fair and wanted to know more. As I described his knowledge, she was pleased. I asked her if I was wrong to pursue this course of action. She said "No! You need to continue."

Drusilla also wanted to know what prompted me to seek him out in the first place. I went over the story of the woman who approached me at the psychic fair, recommending I see Charles. I assumed I had already told her about the woman the day of the fair.

In response, Drusilla said, "You never told me about her that day! You only said to stay away from him! Have you seen her in the classes?"

"No. I've looked for her, but she has never been there."

As time went by, I kept looking for the woman who had spoken so favorably of Charles. Had it not been for her, I would have never sought him out.

One day, I was out with friends I had met in Charles's class. We were discussing how we had each come to know Charles. As I reflected on the woman at the psychic fair, I said to my friends, "It's really weird, but I have never seen that woman again. She said she attended his classes, yet I have been to every class since June, and she has never been there. I have also never seen her at another psychic fair, although I have been looking for her to thank her. I wonder where she is."

One of the friends—extremely intuitive herself—said to me, "She was an angel."

As she said the words, it clicked. I knew immediately that this was so. It now made sense; some higher power had sent me to him.

Ironically, the friend's name who made this connection was Angel. She went on to say, "She is there. You just haven't noticed her."

Yes, there are angels living among us. Sometimes they choose to be seen, other times they are hidden. But if we allow it, we all can witness their help, guiding us toward a more constructive path. Thankfully, I permitted a most noteworthy angel to enter my life. He would support my effort, helping me allow all the goodness of the universe to come my way. His name is Charles Crooks.

Chapter 27

Connections

Going to the psychic fair in early February 2007 not only brought Charles into my life, it also brought a renewed interest in numerology. When I was in college, I studied numerology, but I abandoned my powerful connection to this art because of outside influence. Nevertheless, in 2007, since I could no longer hide my intense curiosity in mysticism, my interest in numerology and other healing modalities resurfaced. As I was studying other spiritual aspects with Charles, they all just seemed to fit in with the greater mysteries of life.

Despite what others had taught me all my life, I instinctively knew it was as if God, not the Devil, was speaking to me. It did not make sense for the Devil or another malevolent being to be providing these insights. Why would an evil presence want to help humanity? I could no longer believe these other methods were destructive systems, as I was taught.

In numerology, numbers have spiritual meaning, providing much about a person's destiny, or life goals, and personality. Some of the things most frequently determined by a numerologist are one's Life Path, Destiny, Soul-Urge, Birthday, Reality, and Personality.

Numerology answers some fundamental questions we all have posed to ourselves at some point in our lives. Who do you think it is that defines your own world? Is it yourself? Or perhaps is it really God working within you?

Think back to the actual concepts of Jesus. Did he not impart knowledge that God lives within every one of us? Destiny, vis-à-vis numerology, simply supports this premise; God does indeed live within each one of us.

When I began to research my own numerological data, I was astounded at some of the information I uncovered. It seemed the data I found had some deeper meaning; this could not be a coincidence.

For instance, I was born on February 23, 1957, into a family of seven children. It was actually extraordinary that my parents were even able to have seven full-term children, because of the little known Rh factor blood type incompatibility between the two of them.

Every person has a blood type, such as O, A, B, or AB, but he or she also has an Rh factor in his or her blood.

Most people have a positive Rh factor. However, between 6 and 7 percent of the U.S. population has a negative Rh factor.

If a child is conceived, in such a case of Rh incompatibility, where the father is Rh factor positive and the mother is Rh factor negative, a big problem for the fetus can develop. While there is little danger for the fetus during the first pregnancy, by the second pregnancy, stillbirth may result. Today, an injection of human immune globulin into the mother within seventy-two hours of delivery can prevent any problems from occurring with the next pregnancy. However, this injection was not available when my mom gave birth to each of us.

Remarkably, although the odds were against it, all seven children miraculously had a negative Rh factor. Therefore, my siblings and I did not have any incompatibility with our mother while she was carrying each of us. My parents were able to have seven full-term children, despite the probability for failure.

In the Bible and in numerology, seven is a divine number. I found it apropos that at the age of seven I became interested in numbers. To me, it appeared I was destined to lead a spiritual path.

As I continued, I made another startling connection, which provided validation that I was on target with my studies. As I meditated, I felt compelled to make a list of all the life-changing events that had happened in my life from the time I was born. These were things that had rocked my world, made me look deeper, ask questions, or change directions in my life. After I made an inventory, I noticed the numbers connection.

Unexpectedly, there were eleven life-changing events on the list, beginning the year my rape occurred and ending at age forty-seven—an eleven-numeral age. Furthermore,

I did not discover and authenticate this information until age fifty—a five-numeral age. My Life Path number is 11. My Soul-Urge number is 9. My Destiny, Personality, and Birthday, expressed as a single-digit number, all equal 5.

The Life Path characterizes the road one currently is travelling and the nature of the journey; the record only included eleven events. The Soul-Urge is the purpose for one's actions; this corroborated my unconscious war with my mother and my weight gain, because a man raped me when I was nine. Finally, one's Destiny is your life's target or spiritual mission—proving to me, beyond a reasonable doubt, that I was on target at age fifty when I began to study the mystical path. The meaning of each number gave even further proof of a higher power working behind the scenes, as these connections could not be an accident.

I made another finding. Of the eleven events I had recorded, there were exactly seven events that were life threatening. These events varied, and any one of them could have caused my demise. As I once stated, seven is a divine number in the Bible and in numerology. To me, this necessitated that I had to die (in a sense) seven times, before I would begin to work the process for a spiritual awakening.

Looking at each of the ages that the eleven events occurred, there is an uncanny, observable fact. In every case except one, they occurred during a five-, seven-, eight-, nine- or eleven-numeral age. This was significant to me, as these numbers were my own primary, personal numerological data. My Destiny, Personality, and Birthday numbers all equal 5; my Reality number is 7; the value of my full first name is 8; my Soul-Urge number is 9; and my Life Path number is 11. The numerical traits associated with each numeral age, during each event, provided further proof the path that I was on determined my purpose. This I could not deny.

As far as the one case that was not a five-, seven-, eight-, nine-, or eleven-numeral age, the event occurred at a one-numeral age. In numerology, Challenges are periods that supply information about obstacles to one's progression during life. Each of us experiences four Challenge periods in life. During the time of this one-numeral age event, I happened to be right in the middle of the only one-numeral Challenge period occurring in my lifetime.

This one-numeral age event tied back to my father, since his birthday number was a one-numeral age also. The event was my nervous breakdown and had to do with dealing with power and men. It was a direct reflection on my attitudes towards my father, who, through his inappropriate actions, caused a blockage to my life's enjoyment. Because of the obstruction, I was attracting the non-constructive influence of the number 1, including others who were overly assertive and aggressive, dominating and willful.

These traits were present a great deal of the time when I experienced that downward spiral into a breakdown. I had been working fiendishly at my company, begging my boss for help. He exhibited the non-constructive traits of the number 1. Another reason for the illness had to do with the ending of a relationship with a man who also manifested these same non-constructive attributes of domination, willfulness, and aggressiveness.

I experienced only one event at a seven-numeral age (my Reality number). Reality numbers generally give advice for age forty and beyond. This one seven-numeral age event happened to be when I had melanoma, the most deadly form of skin cancer. At the time, I was exactly forty-three years old. In fact, I had the melanoma removed on my forty-third birthday. When you add 4 and 3 together, you end up with my Reality number.

This experience related back to my father, whose first-name value was also a 7. He died of cancer at age sixty-one. If you add my dad's age at the date of his death, you again get my Reality number, as 6 plus 1 equals 7. This was another validation that there was purpose for my life. Otherwise, the doctors would not have discovered the melanoma, and I would have died, like my father. Of course, until I began to change my reality at age fifty, I did not make any of these connections. The number of years between age forty-three and fifty is exactly my Reality number. This must be more than happenstance!

Since the discovery of my melanoma, I have been cancer free, and I expect to be cancer free for the remainder of my life. My Reality number was, literally my reality changed!

The number 7 renders several non-constructive vibrations, including hidden motives and suspicions, isolation, and being overly upset by distractions. All of these forces were occurring in my life at the time of the discovery of my cancer. This was primarily due to two reasons. One, my sister-in-law was dying from breast cancer. I was very distraught over her well-being and concerned for my brother and their children. In the meantime, I was having health issues of my own, and I was trying to keep these to myself in order to lessen the emotional load on the family. Due to my sister-in-law's impending death, and because of my motivation to keep my health problems concealed, I felt isolated. These were non-constructive 7 traits.

There were exactly two events on my list involving surgery, but neither were life threatening. Both of these occurred at an eight-numeral age. The value of my first name is 8.

When these two events occurred, I was exhibiting non-constructive 8 traits. I was overworked and stressing out, as a direct result of my job.

The constructive influence of the number 8 has to do with executive ability and character, power and authority, decision and command, and working for a cause. These are all characteristics needed for carrying out the demands of a job. Only when I began working too hard, did I start to display the non-constructive vibrations of the number 8. I wreaked havoc on my own life and had to pay the consequences.

For instance, one eight-numeral age event resulted from too much tension and overwork, making me begin to clench my teeth. Over time, I developed temperomandibular joint disorder, more commonly known as TMJ. In 2001, tedious typing on the computer, added to a twenty-year history of the rhythmic adding of numbers on a ten-key calculator, eventually took a toll on my body. I developed both carpal tunnel syndrome and ulnar nerve compression in both arms. An orthopedic surgeon diagnosed me with these two conditions in the fall of that year.

In another pattern, some events on my list were associated around a nine-numeral age. Exactly three events happened at such nine-numeral ages: a man raped me, I went through a horrific breakup with a long-term boyfriend, and I suffered pneumonia. Incidentally, I was forty-five when I had pneumonia, and the time I spent off work, due to the illness, was four days in the hospital, plus five months of recuperating at my home. Adding 4 plus 5, in both cases, results in the nine-numeral age.

Since 9 is my Soul-Urge number, it represents my inner self, the purpose for my actions. The number 9, being the expression for benefitting humankind, can be an expression of love. If love is an expression of God, who can rightfully claim that God is dead?

In each of the three aforementioned nine-numeral age cases, there was a twofold connotation presenting itself, both constructive and non-constructive.

The first meaning was from the constructive vibrations of the number 9: humanitarian instincts, a giving nature, doing good works, being friendly and congenial, and an attitude of selflessness. In all three events, I could see the connection to this number and its vibrations.

For instance, I was helping the man who raped me find his cat when I was raped, a selfless and congenial act. I did not know the man, and still I helped him. Though I was under a deadline to finish my paper route by a certain time, I took the time to assist this man. The humanitarian instinct in me had stirred me to action.

In the case of my breakup with my longtime boyfriend, again the constructive influence of the number 9 prevailed: namely, a giving nature. I had given all of my heart to this man, which was the primary reason our breakup was so devastating.

Lastly, I saw the number 9 vibration when I experienced pneumonia. At the time, I was spending an inordinate amount of time training an associate in the office. This particular associate was having trouble grasping concepts, and I was taking extra care with him. I exhibited the strong influence of the number 9 while administering to this associate: being friendly, congenial, giving, and caring.

After noting the constructive influences of the number 9 in all three events, the second meaning was from the non-constructive influence of the number 9—possessiveness. In every case of the nine-numeral age events, this non-constructive vibration was forced upon me.

During my rape, the man possessed me. When I was dating my longtime boyfriend, he hid things from me—using this to dominate and control me, which resulted in our breakup. When I contracted pneumonia, the associate I was helping continually stole my time from other associates and other projects.

Still another pattern had events lingering around an eleven-numeral age: my near drowning, my mugging, and the discovery of a rare but lifelong, serious disease. All three eleven-numeral age events required the action of someone else for me to survive. The non-constructive attributes for the number eleven apply in all three of these events: drowning in detail, fear, depression, shyness, timidity, and self-consciousness.

When I almost drowned, I felt the non-constructive vibration of fear, not to mention the part of—literally—drowning in detail. I was worried about the details of finishing the routine swimming test I was taking and ignored my exhaustion. An attending lifeguard rescued me from the bottom of the pool.

In the situation of my mugging, fear was again operating as well as self-consciousness. I had parked in an obscure, abandoned parking lot after working very late. As I rushed to my car, I was fearful of the man following me and self-conscious of my surroundings. I was at the mercy of someone else to survive. The mugger could have easily pulled the trigger of his gun. Thankfully, he did not.

In the case of the diagnosis of a serious, life-altering disease, both depression and self-consciousness were the non-constructive traits in play. I had been depressed before the diagnosis because I had been sick for a quite some time. In addition, I was becoming more and more self-conscious of my health issues, because they affected my job and social activities.

I was dependent on several people to be able to survive this final trial. Close friends and family kept my spirits alive, effectively rescuing me from causing serious harm to myself. In addition, it was a miracle the doctors even diagnosed me correctly. I later found out that it takes, on average, almost ten years for most doctors to diagnose people with an immune deficiency disease like mine. Much of the time, doctors never diagnose these patients accurately, causing early death because of the non-response of the body to infection. However, I was drawn to an outstanding doctor who kept digging to uncover the reasons for my numerous illnesses. I was dependent on a good doctor being able to diagnose the problem.

Remarkably, the most amazing influence of the number 11 is one of spirituality. I now know that all three of these events happened in order for me to open myself to a more spiritual path. This is especially true, considering these three events were outside my control; I was dependent on outside forces to support me.

Only one event took place at a five-numeral age—a neurologist diagnosed me with a seizure disorder. Curiously, the non-constructive vibrations for the number 5 are many of the symptoms for someone who has epilepsy: impatience, edgy temperament and speech, restlessness, discontentment, dissatisfaction, and lacking application.

However, operating under the constructive influence of that same number provides a much different aspect: new and visionary ideas, curiosity, exploration, quick thinking, expansiveness, versatility, promotional tendencies, and being action oriented. In addition, a 5 vibration focuses on enlightenment and forward thinking that will benefit humankind.

As these events transpired in my life, I did take note of their seriousness but did not really grasp the concepts on these traits until I was fifty, a five-numeral age. This was my Destiny number, representing my spiritual mission in life. To me, this was one of the most profound confirmations of my divine connection.

Chapter 28

Part of the Whole

My mother tried to "save" me by raising me in a devout Catholic background. She is a strict Catholic who faithfully goes to church every Sunday, even though her husband did not attend church. She also said her rosary every day before she went to work or got any of us up to go to school and still does, first thing every morning. She considers herself a Christian woman and expected the same of her children.

While I do not regret that upbringing, I have since found out why religion only made me angrier. It was because the Church dictated that God was separate and outside of me. Most religions, it appears, teach this philosophy.

All my life, I have been searching for certain truths. I initially left the Catholic faith because I was not happy with the priest interpreting the Bible for me. It seemed the priest had his own agenda and pushed his philosophy on his congregation during Sunday sermons. I was expected to take his word that his understanding of the Bible was correct. I was a puppet parishioner, and not expected to think on my own. Well, phooey to that! I have always felt that God speaks to each of us directly. We do not need another person to tell us what God intends for us.

My mother made it excruciatingly clear that each of her children should remain faithful to Catholic doctrine. Therefore, it was not an easy decision for me to go against her wishes. The day I announced to her that I would be leaving the Church, just as I had expected, she pitched a fit. She told me quite plainly that I would be going to hell for my actions, laying another guilt trip on me. Although painful, it did not work. I needed something more than guilt to keep me practicing Catholicism.

Therefore, I left the Catholic Church. Over time, I went from church to church, searching for a religion that could meet my needs. Each new church filled the void temporarily. However, within a short time, I felt empty and unfulfilled, as though something was missing.

I did not know it at the time, but my dissatisfaction with each religion stemmed from one fact. Every church I attended kept telling me, "You cannot enter the kingdom of God, unless you are saved." You must be saved, you must be saved! Over and over, I heard this phrase, declaiming an action from a source entirely from outside of me.

The definition of "save," provides the following descriptions: redeem; to put aside; to rescue; to secure and accept; and retrieve. The word "redeem" renders the meaning "to regain." Does not "regain" mean that you must get back to something from which you have separated? If you are "putting aside," are you not separating yourself from something? The other definitions listed above all suggest one of these conditions, implying that one must go outside of oneself in order to be saved.

If the kingdom of God is outside of you, then you are, undeniably, separate from it and from God. However, the light of God is not outside of me, but encompasses all, including the inside of me. He spoke to me every time I received that little intuitive flash of light. Jesus himself spoke of such a fact when he said, "The kingdom of God is within you," (Luke 17:21 KJV). Jesus validated that God was not apart from us.

I never really understood why I was ambivalent towards religion, until I met Charles. One of his most prolific quotes is, "You are not separate, but are part of the whole." It all made sense. When you think of separation, you think of disconnection.

Revelation 19:6 (KJV) says, "For the Lord God omnipotent reigneth." The original Greek word for "omnipotent," as used in this verse, is *pantokrator*, derived from two Greek words, *pas* and *kratos*. These words mean "whole" and "power and strength," respectively. Therefore, one can discern the intention of the original author of this verse, written approximately two thousand years ago. Since God is whole, he encompasses all, including you and me. I do agree with this principle.

The Church and many other structured religions appear to teach this same idea. Based upon the Bible, those systems speak truthfully about this concept but do not validate the entire truth. It is truth with a veil. Just think about it for a moment. There is a paradox, which the Church and others seem to imply, that the spirit of God is entirely outside of us. If God is everywhere, as they appear to teach, how can He be outside of us? The two foundations do not mix and do not make sense to me.

Most everyone will probably concur that a person not only has a physical body, but also consists of another part, the inner spirit. Many people refer to this as our soul. Just about every religion speaks of our soul or inner spirit. Most religions believe and teach that this part will be reconnected to a greater, divine being, known as the Creator, once we die. However, as shown before, if God is also within us, how can we be separate and in need of reconnection? We were never disconnected in the first place! Since God is a part of us, we are a part of God.

Since we have always been, and will continue to be, a part of the whole, or part of God, all answers lie within each of us—not somewhere out in space! As Charles has said, "We simply need to bring them forward." When you use your intuition, you are accessing those answers from the light residing inside of you.

Skeptics might say that intuition is just a person's imagination. I once asked Charles what the difference between intuition and just plain old imagination was. His answer was legitimate. He said, "Intuition is information you receive that is not expected." The word "unexpected" resonated strongly with me.

All my life, I felt there were events that were out of my control, unexpected. As each incident unfolded, I was not always pleased, as many were very turbulent. Furthermore, the answers were also unexpected. As time passed, I realized the change in me that occurred because of the circumstances, turned out to lead me to a more beneficial direction. Remember the phrase, "When God closes a door, he opens a window"? That is just another way to say that something good always came out of what I perceived was a bad condition.

A good example was the situation when I finally moved out of my mom's house at age thirty-seven. I was encouraged by a psychiatrist to move, in order to heal more successfully, after experiencing deep depression that spiraled down into a nervous breakdown. Not only was the nervous breakdown sudden and unexpected, so was the request to move to another address.

I was not happy about the situation and it took several months of persuasion before I finally acted. When I did, I thought I would have trouble finding a suitable house for my little doggies. Amazingly, within a few short days, I found one. It was off the beaten path, in a never-before-seen, secluded neighborhood, and I had only driven down the street because of a gut feeling. As I looked at the house, it felt right.

Although the property owner indicated over the phone that she had an aversion to renting to anyone with dogs, she immediately dismissed that dislike after meeting with me. As we spoke, we discovered we had a mutual friend in common. What are the chances of that happening in a large city like Dallas? With this knowledge, the deal was sealed. I was shocked!

Shortly after moving into the home, I saw an improvement in my health. The doctor had been correct. Moving was necessary, but, ultimately, it was not the doctor who was encouraging me to move, it was my inner light. I would not have even found the place, had I not acted on an unexpected feeling.

Charles also passed on the knowledge that since we are part of the whole, there is both light and darkness within each one of us. We can choose to manifest either one, whether light, by the constructive attributes, or darkness, by the non-constructive attributes. Whatever we give attention to, becomes. It is our choice.

As an example, Charles has referred to a story about Mother Teresa. Once, she was asked to go to an anti-war demonstration. Her reply was, "If you want me to go to a peace demonstration, I will go. However, I will not attend an anti-war demonstration." Charles explained her response. Mother Teresa understood that by giving power to an anti-war demonstration, there must be a war to demonstrate against. By focusing on a peace demonstration, she brought peace to the forefront, supporting its nature.

Have you ever thought about where our spirit actually resides? I have. It has to be somewhere in us, but where? Charles talks about the breath of life quite a bit. He asks, "What is the component of breath that we find so valuable to ourselves?"

The vital life force is a concept often discussed and many times portrayed in various forms in movies. Do you suppose our breath contains this force? Could the vital life force include the spirit of God, whose light encompasses all?

When we are born, until we take our first breath, we are lifeless. Without that breath, there would only be an unresponsive, physical body. This is why breathing is induced by some means immediately after birth if we do not begin to breathe on our own. It may be as simple as cutting the umbilical cord or slapping the baby on the butt. Since every human consists of both a physical body and God's light, it is easy to conclude that breath contains not only our self and character, but also the light of God within.

Words of John 4:24 (KJV) give solid evidence to support this fact: "God is a Spirit." The original Greek word for "spirit," used in this verse, is pneuma, which literally means "breath" or "current of air."

Since the breath is life, we can deduce that life is a component of our breath. However, how does one define life? The dictionary's definition is "existence" or "vitality," but what exactly gives us vitality or brings us into existence?

Charles asserts that the breath consists of multiple components. Most everyone would agree that one of these components is the various gases required to allow the body to function on a physical level.

We have already established that God is everywhere, including living within us. We have determined that breath contains life, and that without breath, there is only a physical body. Therefore, does it not stand by reason that God may live within our breath?

Referring back to everything we have been taught about God, some of the attributes most commonly associated with Him are love and light: "For God is love," (1 John 4:8 KJV) and "Father of lights," (James 1:17 KJV).

Therefore, as quoted from Charles, "Would it be reasonable to determine that some of the components of the breath would be unconditional love and that all-expanding light that seems to bind us all together in one form or another?"

Love is the answer, for without the love-containing breath, we cannot live in the physical world!

So what is life? Since light and love are the divine components of the breath, and since the breath is life, and life is simply the product of unconditional love and light, our very existence is based on the light of God, who is love and life. As Charles has said, "They are manifestations from our greater selves to the world." Furthermore, since the source of these manifestations lie within, "we are carriers of light, love, and life." Did I have love? Yes, since God is love and since His spirit is a part of me!

Charles further insists that the breath "is so dear that we take any action to be able to maintain it," as it is vital for life. Yet, he argues, the breath is so familiar that we no longer give attention to it. We take it for granted.

He says no matter where you are, as long as you are breathing, there is life and therefore, there is love and light in you. This is a fact, whether a person likes it or not. As Charles likes to say, "We are all stuck with it." A person could try to deny this fact and hide in the deepest, darkest cave. It is his choice, but he still will not be outside of the light of God, for each breath one takes is an unanticipated and realized acceptance that he is part of the whole and not separated from it. What is real existence? It is being in the light of God, for we cannot hide from it, no matter what.

Since both light and dark lie within, we each have a choice. Which attributes do we want to promote? We can choose to advance the constructive attributes of light or the unconstructive attributes of darkness. Charles asserts that love, understanding, compassion, honor, honesty, and humility are the constructive attributes. To promote the good attributes, all we have to do is bring them forward. It is our right.

The unconstructive attributes are simply the opposite of the good ones: judgment, hate, insensitivity, cruelty, dishonor, dishonesty, and arrogance. When you judge, you are placing yourself either above or below. That is, in either a superior or inferior position. Since we are part of the whole, all parts are connected and equal. Therefore, when you judge you are considering yourself separate from the whole; you are limiting your natural characteristics by not placing yourself in a neutral position. The bottom line is: being equal is the easiest!

Because judgment causes one to feel separate and not equal, it will give the illusion that something is lacking. A person seeks acceptance from others to replace what he perceives is missing. He tries to gain acceptance by either exercising power or by placing himself in a weaker position than others.

Judgment is a state of domination, either over others or by others, which shows that, as Charles says, "Judgment is not a spiritual process, but rather a process of slavery that turns one away from the light within and towards the darker path."

For an individual to know anything about a divine being, he generally has always relied on getting the information from someone else directly. Our parents, teachers, friends, structured religious systems, and our individual experiences all teach us patterns and behaviors that can be non-constructive. It does not matter. The point is that when this happens, we become dependent on that source. Before long, we are preconditioned to use judgment.

Our truth about ourselves is based upon what has been told to us, allowing us to become inferior to it, but inferiority is an act of slavery and judgment.

What is the solution? Charles suggests a more beneficial approach to understanding ourselves and our spiritual connection. That key lies in the form of observation and validation. Instead of relying on others for the answers, it is beneficial to base our truth upon something we have proven for ourselves, using a more scientific approach for discerning the truth. When we observe what is presented to us without bias, and then test that information for ourselves, we can be assured it is true. Don't just take someone else's word for it; validate all aspects of what is being presented!

When undergoing a scientific experiment, you observe with a complete, whole model as your measure. You accept all the parts. Therefore, everything is part of the whole, and nothing is separate. Everything is equal.

Through observation, we permit ourselves to see that all things, including the light of God, are part of ourselves. As Charles teaches, in this scientific way, "We can find the whole of all things that are within every one of us. If we wish to bring forward a constructive action, concept, or ideal," we may, if we so choose. "It is not outside of us. It is a matter of giving permissions to allow these great attributes existing within us now to come forward."

When I began my journey with Charles, it was apparent that he was psychic. He knew things about me that he could not have known unless he had used his intuition. This intuition stems from the light of God that exists everywhere.

As I continued attending Charles's classes, it became clear to me that I was on a journey of self-awareness. Charles has always stated that the answers lie within each of us. He does not give those answers. He simply provides the tools by which others can seek their own truth, allowing each individual the opportunity to discover who they are, in their own time.

Since everyone is different, we cannot compare ourselves with someone else, assuming our journey will be the same, or even that it will occur at the same rate. This would be judgment. Instead, it is beneficial for each of us to acknowledge we are all on a journey, designed specifically and individually from the spirit.

I once said to Charles, "I wish I had met you thirty years ago." His response was, "You met me when you chose to meet me."

This is because the divine within knows the moment each individual is ready to make the journey to spiritual enlightenment.

Charles did not dictate what my truth was, and he never judged. I have often shared my intuitive thoughts and visions from my dreams and meditations with Charles. I expected him to give me all the answers, telling me what the dream or vision meant. I was dismayed to discover that he did not do this. Instead, he asked, "What do you think it means?" I told him what I felt it indicated, but he still did not give me more information. He only offered words of encouragement such as "excellent" or "very good." One of his favorite lines is: "Not to worry, you are on target." I could always tell that he knew more but was holding back. I often expressed my frustration with him, but he never budged. It drove me nuts!

With time, I finally understood why he did not give me all the answers. When we begin to unlock the truth, not all the answers to every single question come flooding into our consciousness at one time. Instead, the spirit provides bits and pieces of the information as we can handle it. Everyone has heard the line, "You are never given more than you can handle." That quote applies with spiritual enlightenment.

Even though Charles may know the entire truth, he does not presume to tell an individual what the complete truth is. To do so, he would be putting himself in a superior position and would be in judgment. Instead, he lets all those he supports find out the truth by themselves, through observation and testing. Charles's short comments are intended to empower not frustrate.

It is important that we not only observe but also test the information we receive, either overtly or subtly. To do so provides us with the fact that the knowledge and/or process of enlightenment are ours alone. They are not someone else's.

In my own journey, I know the information I received is true because I have tested it. I no longer simply believe what I am told. For instance, I have tested and verified truths using numerology, as previously outlined in this book. I have also tested and verified information received using other means, such as the validity of my intuition and other methods not outlined here. Since I have discovered certain truths about myself on my own and have not relied on the Church or anyone else for them, no one can take them away from me. They are my truths, validated by my diagnosis.

I am not upset with others for their current perceptions of who they are, for this itself would be judgment. Instead, it is beneficial for me to allow everyone the option to make a choice. Just as Charles allowed me to seek my own truth; it is not my intention to tell others what their own truth is.

Charles does not like the word "should." One of the first things he said to me when I met him was, "Take 'should' out of your vocabulary because 'should' implies you know better than someone else, suggesting you are superior, and this is judgment."

I know what he said was true. Whenever someone in my life told me that I "should" do something, there was resistance. It was the very reason that I became angry. When I first got sick, I cannot tell you how many people said to me, "You should be reading your Bible." It did not matter that I was already reading it, the fact they assumed I was not, made me angry. The result: I stopped reading it! Because of their judgmental attitude, I did the opposite as an act of rebellion.

Total strangers have even given me unsolicited should advice. The most egregious case was when a flight attendant, after seeing splints on both my wrists for carpal tunnel syndrome, forcefully stated, "You should be taking vitamin B6."

I wanted to ignore her, but my anger flared as I had not asked her advice, and I had already tried that suggested remedy, and it did not work. When I informed her of this, she made matters worse.

"Oh no! You didn't take enough. You should have taken more!" She had no idea how much I had taken. I was offended by her arrogance, her assuming I did not know what I was doing.

I now attempt to refrain from using the word "should" in my vocabulary. It is not easy, and I constantly have to make an effort. However, since I have chosen to work a constructive, spiritual path, there can be no other way.

I am not telling others that they should do such and such. I am simply stating the facts that have applied to me. If an individual finds it beneficial to work a constructive path, so be it. It is in this way that I am free in giving towards others and promoting the constructive attributes of humanity.

Since everything lies within our reach, we can choose to either advance good or bad. How do we do this? It is simply done by directing our thoughts to those attributes that we wish to promote. Charles says that "if you feel something is beyond or outside of you, you are telling the universe that you do not have it." The universe responds directly and conforms to your reality.

For instance, if you want wealth, think of wealth with all of your being, as if you already had it, and you shall obtain it. However, if you think about riches in the context of missing it, you are in fact focusing on lack of prosperity, and you will continue to be absent of wealth in your life.

Since our very existence is based upon light, I have chosen to bring forward the good inside of me. I devote my attention to those things that have been shown to be the most desirable qualities exhibited by any human. These are love, understanding, compassion, honor, honesty, and humility.

However, before I could redirect my thoughts completely, destructive emotions had to be released. No one could tell me when or how to do so, not even Charles. Instead, I had to let go of the emotions, in my own time and by myself. Charles helped facilitate the release, but he could not do anything without my permission. It was only when I felt safe, a recommendation by Charles, that I could allow myself to begin to release these destructive emotions.

During the first private session with Charles, he told me I needed to release old emotional baggage. One of the very first things Charles said to me when I met him at the psychic fair was that I was not at fault. At the time, I did not know what he what he was talking about. I was blaming myself for my terrible childhood experiences. Later, I learned part of this emotional baggage and blame had to do with continuing a war with my mother for her inadequate handling of the events surrounding my rape.

Like most children, I began calling my mother "Mom" or "Mommy" when I first learned to talk. I continued calling her these names until soon after my rape, when I started calling her "Mother," despite the fact that no one else in my family called her by this moniker.

When asked why I called her "Mother" instead of "Mom" or "Mommy" by numerous friends, I simply replied, "She's my mother, isn't she? Besides, 'Mother' is much more referential, don't you think?" They just looked at me queerly and dropped the subject.

Actually, it was a subconscious decision on my part to call my mom by this seemingly distant name. I was not even aware that I had begun calling her something different until others poignantly pointed it out to me. Despite others' questions, I continued calling her Mother for forty plus years. It would take the shaman, Charles Crooks, to change all that.

He helped me understand that the day my mom hushed our household, she also hushed my emotions. It was no coincidence that I began calling her Mother the day of my rape. Until I learned to release my destructive emotions and cry real tears, I would not be able to call her Mom.

Chapter 29

Listening to Instincts

From the moment we are born, two parts of us compete for our attention. It is the oldest struggle in the universe. One is the intellect and the other is our inner self, also known as the spirit or soul. The intellect's main job is to protect the body at all costs, so an individual can function in this world. It does this by using the five senses of taste, smell, sight, hearing, and feeling. The intellect represents the physical side of oneself. The sixth sense, or your intuition, corresponds to the ethereal side of you, your spirit or soul. The spirit encompasses everything, whereas the intellect only covers your physical being. While the intellect can die, the spirit lives on forever.

When we are born, the intellect takes control quickly. Satisfying one of our first basic urges when we enter the world, hunger, can provide a good reason for this phenomenon. When the request for food is made, the intellect, being a baby and new to the world, looks to the spirit to handle the situation. However, since the spirit is connected to all things and knows it will always be part of the whole, it is secure without lunch. Essentially, the spirit says to the intellect, "Hey man, I have everything I need. I do not need food to live. You handle it, since you are so worried about it." The spirit defers the task to the intellect.

The intellect, whose primary focus is to protect the body, takes the necessary action and by crying, obtains food for the individual. As this scenario repeats itself, it soon appears to the intellect that the spirit is totally useless and the intellect begins its rule.

However, the spirit is not absent. The spirit is just very secure with its continued existence. It is always present and sometimes sends messages out on its own, in the form of intuition, despite resistance from the intellect, which now thinks it is in control. Whether we find it beneficial to listen to the spirit is another matter. Some people call intuition a third eye because, instead of a voice, they actually can see things outside the five senses.

When a strange man raped me, the spirit sent a message to me. However, I did not recognize it until I began writing this book at age fifty. The message was that my spirit would not begin to ascend until I was fifty.

I made the connection as I wrote the words, "Do not move until you count to fifty . . . then you can get up . . .

and go home," while writing this book. Those words were describing the instructions from my rapist after the act.

However, they also provided a direct commentary on my exact age when I would be able to move forward, "rising" and going "home" to the truth. Of course, it turned out that fifty was precisely the age when that defining moment occurred in my spiritual ascension. I wasn't listening at age nine, but now I understand. It was another validation of a higher power working beyond my physical sight. It was God within me. Even though I thought I was abandoned when I was raped, He never left.

Although I know we all have intuitive faculties, I now recognize that the more trials we encounter in our lives, the more developed this third eye becomes. This is because when the intellect has reached its limits, due to some trauma or overload, it shuts down, allowing our intuition to work without resistance.

The horrific things that happened in my childhood caused my intuition to become more pronounced. I went through extreme adversity, so that my intellect would be more likely to defer to the spirit. It was very difficult to endure the hardships in my life. However, those trials were necessary in order to develop my spiritual being more fully and ascend to a higher level.

Therefore, I feel blessed for all the experiences in my life, the good as well as the bad. All my adversities turned out, in the long run, to be a gift.

My mom also has strong intuitive talents, since she suffered with similar issues in her childhood and because of the hardships of living with my father and raising a large family. For instance, my mom could tell when her sister was coming for a visit before she had announced the intention. My mom said, "I would just get a feeling the kinfolk were headed our way." In addition, many times she knew who was on the phone before she actually picked it up.

I have been known for this same distinction, knowing who was on the phone before answering. Others witnessed this ability in me. At work, I used to amaze an associate who worked directly across the hall with my ability.

I trained extensively at the time and usually had someone in my office when the phone would ring. Before I picked it up, I would say to the trainee, "Excuse me. Let me get this. It's . . . ," announcing who was on the phone. I was usually correct in my assumption. The phone had no caller ID, and therefore, it was impossible for my intellect to tell who was calling beforehand.

The associate across the hall had the habit of listening in on my conversations. He often bounced over after I had been talking to someone to comment on the dialogue. Because of his actions, I thought he had the biggest mickey-mouse ears. Nothing eluded him.

One afternoon, after hearing me mention the identity of the caller before I picked up the phone, he came racing over after I finished my chat and asked, "How do you know who is on the phone when you haven't even picked it up? You seem to always know who it is on the other line!" I simply told him, "I can tell by the sound of the ring."

It was true. I could discern the uniqueness of the caller by the tone of the ring. I associated different tones with different callers. Sometimes I could make a distinction just by a gut feeling or picture in my mind. This revelation awed my coworker, as there was only one physical ringtone on the phone. However, my inner voice heard more ringtones than were possible in the physical world.

Not only had I developed the talent of intuition to a greater degree than I would have had I not experienced so many hardships, but also whenever I did not listen to my instincts, I often experienced more severe suffering. It was a nudge from my inner self to put me back on the path more beneficial for my life. Sometimes, it took a more drastic knock over the head to stop me from totally ignoring my gut instincts.

For instance, by the time I had reached age forty-seven, the spirit had sent many clear signals to leave my job and change directions. I just was not listening. Thus, I was smacked across the face with a loud message before I finally listened and responded.

The message came in the form of a devastating illness. It made me unable to work, forcing me to leave my position. At the time, I told several people that I knew the illness was God's way of putting me on another path. However, it would take me several more years before I finally acted and got on track. I had to experience the pain of separation and the hardship of my illness, in order for the intellect to finally move over and let the spirit emerge more fully.

The illness required me to separate from everything: coworkers, friends, and family. I felt alone and miserable. It proved to me that sometimes events force a person to consider the separation they feel between themselves and the rest of humanity. By being literally isolated from the world, the universe was driving me to look at that separation. Discovering that separation was heartbreakingly painful. When I was at my lowest point, almost ready to kill myself, the spirit came to my rescue, leading me to seek the truth, which ultimately resulted in finding happiness.

Separation exists only in the intellect. When you feel separation, you feel pain. However, as you discover that you are part of the whole, and that you and the spirit are inseparable, your reality changes. You become happier.

In the past, although I did not always totally ignore my instincts, I never really gave them much thought. I did not fully understand the source of those unexpected impulses. However, now I am paying closer attention to them. As I do so, my instincts become stronger. Charles says that if you focus on something, the universe will "comply, bringing forward that which you give attention to."

In the past, when I did listen to my instincts, it paid off big! Therefore, I know it is the right thing to do.

A good example occurred when I decided to build a house several years ago. I had already decided where I wanted to build. I spent almost a year perusing the community, scoping out the various builders and their developing neighborhoods.

As I drove from builder to builder, checking out their offerings, I was always drawn to the sign of one particular builder. It was located on an empty tract of land. Within a few months, the builder began construction on the site. As soon as the road infrastructure was completed on this site, I began to drive around the developing neighborhood. Each time I drove through it, I felt a tingle of energy.

Within time, I had visited all the builders in the area, except the one builder whose neighborhood so attracted me. I had not visited them because they had not yet situated a model home on the site. However, now it was imperative that I speak with them, so I called the telephone number listed on the sign.

The builder's sales associate answered the phone promptly and gave me directions to the nearest model home. It was only a few miles from the developing community. I drove over to visit with her immediately. The minute I stepped into the model home, I just knew I had found the perfect builder for my home.

As I left the model home that afternoon, my inner voice told me to take another drive over to the neighborhood with which I had become so enamored. Within minutes, I was driving slowly through the neighborhood. Suddenly, a lot jumped out at me. It was a large, vacant lot, adjacent to one of the few houses already built. As I put the car into park, I could see the hand of God, outstretched over the lot.

Without a moment's notice, I picked up my cell phone and called the sales associate again. "I am in my car and looking at a lot. Can you tell me what I need to do to secure this lot?"

After establishing which lot I was referring to, it was confirmed that the lot was available for purchase. I reserved the lot and construction began!

After looking for almost a year, I instantaneously decided to pick a certain lot based on a gut feeling I had. It turned out to be one of the best decisions I ever made. Not only was the construction process thoroughly enjoyable, despite what I had heard to the contrary, but the lot proved the envy of the entire neighborhood.

My lot was the only house in the development that came with a large tree. It was a hackberry tree that I had not even noticed when I called and asked the sales associate about the lot. That was because it looked more like a bush than a tree from my vantage point, as it had never been trimmed. None of the other houses had trees, as the developer, as is typical, had wiped all brush and trees from the landscape in order to make construction easier.

When I chose my floor plan and was in the initial building discussions, I asked the foreman to keep the tree, provided it was not located too close to the house, as that may have caused foundation problems later. As it turned out, there was ample distance from the tree to the house. In fact, the tree is perfectly located, directly in the middle of my backyard.

One day after I purchased the lot, I drove my best friend over to see the future site of my home. As I was showing her the lot, I pointed out the tree. She said, "That's an ugly hackberry tree. Cut that thing down!"

However, I knew better. I told her that even though she thought the tree was an eyesore, she would change her mind after I had it trimmed. After all, it would provide shade, no other property had a tree, and most importantly, it was alive.

Shortly after moving in, I did have the tree trimmed. After pulling off many of the bottom branches, the shape of the tree was fantastic! It is balanced in its branching, has a wonderful canopy of foliage, and is a refuge for wildlife. The birds sing and the squirrels frolic in that tree. I love it and so does Drusilla. She could not believe the change in the tree! Had I not looked beyond what was there, I would not have been blessed with such a wonderful gift.

Many years earlier, I bought a buffet and china cabinet at a rummage sale. I paid three hundred dollars for both pieces. Both of them were very old and weathered. When my sister saw them, she said she would not have given twenty-five dollars for them. I told her to wait until I had refinished the pieces, because the wood was good. I was right. As soon as I refinished them, she could not believe the transformation. I still have both pieces of furniture and often get compliments on them.

Many times, we each make the same mistake. We cannot see what is deep within and therefore we discount the value. We all have common decency within us. We are good. It just takes some trimming, molding, and polishing to bring it out.

Chapter 30

Mother to Mom

Charles showed me that from the time I was very small, I was indoctrinated with the concept that "all things are outside of me, and I must react to them." For instance, if someone wronged me and did not ask for forgiveness, I became angry with them. I was placing myself above them by not being neutral on the issue; I assumed I knew better than they did. I was in a state of judgment.

The early religious instruction I received did not provide any evidence that it was legitimate. Meeting Charles gave me a new understanding of spirituality that has made me whole. By observing and testing the information presented to me, I truly understand that what he conveys is valid. This new knowledge has allowed me to begin to heal and find true happiness.

His concepts were at first foreign to me. However, scientists are discovering things that are invisible to the naked eye every single day. Many of the concepts discussed in this book are actually laws of quantum physics. For instance, our thoughts do actually affect our world and we are all connected. Why is it such a stretch to believe the inner spirit talks to us if we only allow it?

I learned to release the war with my mother. It was not a matter of forgiving her that made the difference. It was the insight that her actions were necessary and, therefore, a gift, in order to bring about a desire to live and work a more constructive path. Because of this adjustment of understanding, I was able to release the emotions associated with my rape and finally cry the tears forbidden so many years before. I no longer refer to my mother as Mother. I now call her Mom.

I began seeing Charles in April 2007. Within several months, I noticed a change in my mom's treatment of me. I became cognizant of it right after we had an explosive argument. She had never before attempted to initiate an apology. I always had to do that. Incredibly, this time, she was the first to apologize. I was amazed!

At the end of July 2007, my mom suddenly began experiencing numerous serious health problems. Her change in attitude was becoming more apparent as the frequency of her favorable responses increased. For one thing, she worried about my health, since her declining health was detrimental to my own, as I was prone to infections. She told me, "Cindy, you take care of yourself. I don't want you to get sick."

She had never worried about my health before. In fact, she so detested going to the doctor, she often hid symptoms from me to refrain from going. When it became obvious that she was in worse shape than she divulged, I insisted she go to the doctor. Despite my fussing and informing her of the consequences of waiting to both her health and mine, she still did not acquiesce. It made me angry, as she was painfully aware that with my fragile immune system, I could easily catch her illness. It was like trying to lift a heavy, loaded truck with two hands; she would not budge. Only after threatening her and, many times, obtaining the assistance of other family members, was I able to get her to comply. So her statement about not wanting me to become ill, as a consequence of her illness, was very profound, indicating something had changed.

Another instance of her changing attitude took place shortly after I began writing in the late summer of 2007. I told my mom that I was writing a book about my rape. I thought she would be upset, especially since it was apparent that the book would include my feelings towards her role in that event. Instead, she told me she wanted my book to be successful. I was happily surprised.

At the end of September 2007, she contracted MRSA, a severe antibiotic-resistant staph infection, during a hospital confinement. Before her hospitalization, she was living with me. Since I had an immune deficiency disorder, my immunologist strongly discouraged her continued living arrangements with me. When it was time to release her from the hospital, she moved in permanently with my sister.

My mom continued with the positive comments, even after her departure from my home. She suddenly began talking about wanting me to meet someone and have a happy life with him. This was in direct contrast to her dialogue and behavior in the past. I know she truly meant it and was sincere in all the comments she had recently made to me.

Within months of working with Charles, my reality began to change and the universe responded. My mom was given the opportunity to nurture me, finally. She did so with success. I have concluded that it was an enlightening experience to spend the many years living in the same household with my mom. It was an experience of healing and knowing her.

La Niña, which means "little girl," is a weather phenomenon characterized by unusually cold temperatures on the surface of certain areas of the ocean. This pattern can have a profound effect on climate, causing raging tropical cyclone activity.

Just as with normal weather patterns, all of us go through storms in our lives. These are opportunities to clear the skies after the rain, chances for renewal. With me, there were many storms. The one most significantly discussed in this book was the one I went through with my mom. It was the La Niña storm of my life, as there were cold emotions of a little girl, which needed neutralizing to stop the rage. It came to a head in 2007, precisely when an actual La Niña weather event unfolded. It would only be a matter of time for the skies to clear.

After a severe storm, cleanup is often required. During these times, the true spirit of humanity lives in those benevolent souls who inevitably come to our rescue. I weathered the storm, but it would take the kindness of another to help me clean up the damage.

After the Katrina Hurricane hit the Gulf Coast of the United States in August 2005, many people lost their homes, causing drastic changes in their lives. In order to survive, these people had to relocate to completely different states of the country.

It is estimated that the hurricane caused over 81 billion dollars in damage, the costliest natural disaster in U.S. history. The catastrophic failure of the levee systems in New Orleans prompted an immediate review of their design and construction. Due to widespread criticism of the way the government handled the storm, an investigation ensued by the U.S. Congress and resulted in personnel changes within the Federal Emergency Management Agency (FEMA).

Using the analogy of the storm, we see that many times we have to change in order to deal with the aftermath of the storm. A similar change was necessary in my life. I needed to redirect my thinking, focusing on the good, happy times in my past and the making of more joyous times ahead. As I looked, I was able to make a list of numerous cheerful times in my life. Despite the hardships, it was not all bad. In fact, I had many good memories.

A number of happy memories involve my mom. When I was young, I always anxiously awaited my mom's return from work. In the late afternoon, I watched intently for her to exit the bus and then ran down the street to greet her. My favorite day of the week was Wednesday, because that was my mom's day off from work. When I was growing up, we never drank sodas. However, if one of us got sick, she would go out and get 7 Up to give us a special treat. My mom decorated a special birthday cake for each one of us on every birthday until we reached adulthood and left home. And one of my most precious memories of my mom was watching her dance to big band music. She has a distinctive dance style that I will always remember. She also always lit up when she talked about stories of her childhood, her parents, her old boyfriends, and my dad.

However, my most cherished memory of my mom is spending time with her while driving across the country together. During my entire childhood, because of the expense, our family only took one family vacation. When I was twelve years old we went to Pennsylvania to visit relatives.

As we drove each day, the scenes passing just outside my window fascinated me. That trip solidified my love of travel. When I was older, I began to travel just as I had imagined during that first trip with my family. Beginning in 1982, I began taking a very satisfying, annual, two-week driving trip with my mom.

She was an excellent travel companion. She read the map and apparently happened to have a knack for this, as we did not get lost once. In addition, she pointed out various land formations and attractions we would be coming across as we journeyed. We trekked across the country, year after year, visiting just about every state in the union in the process.

My mom gave me much delight during these times. It was pure joy sharing the experience with her, seeing the stunning beauty of our country. I am thankful for those memories etched forever into my mind. While traveling, I felt more connected to the universe than I had in my entire life. My travels were some of the most spiritual journeys for me. I always felt revived afterwards.

One thing became very evident though all of this: Despite the pain she had caused me, my mother was one of the most significant blessings in my life. Who cares whether my mom married a divorced man? Who cares if she may not have wanted me to marry? These, like other things, were not for me to judge. Besides, she gave me the things necessary for me to realize my true spiritual worth.

Had she told us about certain aspects of her life, I may not have turned out the way I had. It was necessary for me to examine my life with her, expressing my emotions, in order to allow the spirit to rise. I was blessed to have someone who had a strong belief in God.

Although money was tight, she sacrificed much in order to make sure we had a spiritual education in a private Catholic school, where she thought we could learn to tell right from wrong. She could have very easily sent each of us to public school, saving her hard-earned money for things others may deem more important, but had she not taken the time to educate each of her children about a greater being than ourselves, I might have chosen the dark path.

One of my favorite Christian songs is "Amazing Grace." The words of that song always haunted me, "I once was lost, but now am found, was blind, but now I see." Had it not been for my mom, I may have never heard these words. I now have a renewed sense of their meaning, as it is easy for me to see that "lost" is the same as separated, and to be "found" is the same as choosing my own reality. I was blind, but now I do see!

I think her belief in God provided me with still another gift. All my life, everyone has always told my mom she looked much younger than her years. It is true; she looks at least ten to fifteen years younger than she is. This was true, even when she was experiencing the most trying times in her life. I now know it was not only her strong belief in God but also her allowing the divine light to shine and radiate outward. My mom's youthful exterior is actually a reflection of her everlasting, divine spirit.

All my life, I was unconsciously aware of her light, and I allowed the same light to radiate out from me. This explains why many people also tell me I appear much younger than my actual age. It has turned out that the best anti-age formula is to allow the light to shine. Imagine, since the beginning of time, people have been searching the world for the fountain of youth, but it has been inside of us all along!

Living in such a way not only works as an anti-aging formula, but also it extends one's lifetime. I have noticed that Catholic nuns seem to live into very old age, many of them living to ninety or one hundred, well past the average mortality age for females. Statistics show that married people live longer than single individuals do. But this fails to explain the longevity of nuns.

The answer is simple. They let the light shine. My mom extended her life as nuns do. Both of her parents died soon after turning age seventy. Scientists agree that, genetically, we are a reflection of our parents. Their life expectancies affect our life expectancy.

Lifestyle decisions can also impact mortality age. However, my mom's diet and stress level was not that different from her parents'. As of this writing, my mom has lived longer than her parents did, by more than thirteen years, and is eighty-four years young, even though she lost her lifelong partner almost thirty years ago.

Even though she made some bad choices that seriously affected me, she still had good in her. Yes, I did complain about her. Yes, her choices sometimes reflected the bad. But who among us has not made bad choices? I recognize that the training that she received from others, as well as her own bad experiences, aggravated her decisions and actions. We all have both good and bad within us. We all make errors in judgment. Therefore, I do not blame her for those bad choices. It is not a matter of forgiveness. It is simply the choice to dissolve or release the emotions associated with the errors. After all, she, like all of us, has the light of God in her.

Chapter 31

Allowing God's Energy

All my life I have felt alone. It began when I was an infant in the crib, watching from a distance while others in my family ate pie. I felt like I was not part of the group, and I wanted to be included. It continued throughout my life, exacerbated by the fact that several men sexually assaulted me, which only further isolated me.

I incorrectly blamed my mom. I was never alone. It is impossible to be alone once you realize that you are part of everything and that everything is connected. Although I perceived I was separate and alone, I was not. Therefore, in answer to the question, "Are we alone?" the answer is definitely, "No! We are never alone!"

My inner self steered me all along during my life. I am thankful I was guided towards a sudden intuitive leap of understanding to take action, causing me to begin the process of releasing outdated emotions and discover the truth.

In the process, my health and outlook for the future improved. The improvement began almost immediately after meeting Charles, before I had lost even one pound. I had carpal tunnel syndrome in both my arms. Even though I had surgery, the pain was still significant, requiring me to wear splints twenty-four hours a day. Magically, my carpal tunnel syndrome has completely vanished, despite the fact that my typing has increased.

In addition, my right shoulder had been causing me tremendous pain, a condition that initially began in 2004. Several doctors looked at it, and I went through many hours of physical therapy, but to no avail. By early 2007, the pain was so great, that one of my doctors referred me to a shoulder specialist who, after looking at an MRI of the area, told me that the only way to relieve the pain was through surgery. Fate intervened, and I could not go forward with the surgery immediately due to other factors. In the meantime, I had begun seeing Charles and over a period of several months, the shoulder miraculously stopped hurting, even though I did not have the required surgery.

Other health conditions have also improved significantly. I am no longer depressed. I am confident I will completely heal very soon, despite doctors' opinions. I am happy!

I also benefitted from valuable life lessons and honed skills which will be useful in the next chapter of my life—the chapter relating to helping and supporting the education of others. I learned worthwhile lessons and gained insight into certain life experiences, which afforded me the unique position to offer compassion to others in similar situations.

Even though I initially regretted working long-term for a company where I was unhappy, I later discovered that the skills I learned there were not a waste. Once I understood the concept of the whole, I could comprehend that we are wholly connected and that everything is part of the whole. This includes the good as well as the bad. How can something that comes from God be a waste?

I had the opportunity to practice writing and supporting the education of others during my twenty-four-year tenure with that former employer. These skills were proven valuable when I began writing a book designed specifically to inspire and help others.

Initially I had sought out Charles in order to drop pounds. He did help me in that area. Since working with him, I have been gradually losing weight. Even though the premise for my contacting Charles was to lose something, I gained so much more. It was his love, understanding, compassion, honesty, honor, and humility. He supported me by allowing me to discover that I have them also and that, to be completely happy, it would be beneficial to live by these attributes. In doing so, I can be a beacon for others, drawing them in to the light that we all have available to us. This is my purpose and joy!

To change my whole way of thinking was not an easy thing. I have often told my friends about a theory I have concerning weight. Fat is essentially energy. From the law of conservation of energy we know that energy cannot be destroyed, only transformed. When someone is losing weight, the energy has to go somewhere. I had always assumed it was going to another person, causing him or her to gain weight. At least, it sounded like a good theory.

Energy is involved in the process of losing weight. I did have that part correct. When you think of a stopped-up drain, you can understand why I gained weight. I had blocked my energy of light, causing a backup. When we let the energy flow, the excess weight goes down, releasing the backup.

I used to sit and stand with my arms tightly crossed over my chest. After several classes sitting like this, Charles came over and whispered something in my ear. He said, "There are only two things I want from you. One, do not cross your arms over your chest and, two, sleep like a floozy." Upon hearing his request, I immediately received a mental picture of a woman with her legs opened wide. I would realize later on, that there was no better way to get me to remember to sit with my feet flat on the floor, arms down at my sides, than with such a provocative statement.

I was resisting, blocking the energy, love, and light inside of me. During my first private session with Charles, he told me I had gained weight as a form of protection. It was a safety factor programmed into me as a result of the various hardships in my life. The weight was synonymous with wearing a suit of armor. With the intellect still in control, I had refused to accept the evidence of our true connection to God and the universe.

Life is energy. It is light and love. It is God living within you. When you cross your arms and legs, you are effectively blocking that energy. It is as if you have cut the cable connection. You not only restrict the light and love within you but also the light and love that radiates out from you. By opening ourselves, we are free to receive it and give it. Therefore, Charles's statement to "sleep like a floozy" was instruction on the importance of keeping the energy lines open.

Although other times in my life "opening wide" unnerved me, now I have grown to a deeper appreciation of Charles's motive. I learned: Do not resist. Continue to allow the goodness within you to come to your consciousness by releasing old hurts and redirecting your thoughts to the constructive attributes. This is a lifelong goal and journey.

At the beginning of my very first private session with Charles, back in April 2007, as I took a seat in a chair across from him, he gave me a caveat before he began working. He said that because my involvement mainly required that I just sit while he worked, our time together may appear boring. However, something happened at the very end of the sitting that was so powerful that it has continued to stick with me.

An incredible vision unfolded before my very eyes. It appeared immediately after Charles instructed me to quiet my mind. He wanted me to let my mind wander. I was not sure I would be able to handle the task. However, he suggested I focus my attention on an empty corner of the room and look beyond the blank wall. I gazed at the corner, but at the same time, I instinctively shifted my eyes to a point just off-center of the area.

Within seconds, I saw a rustic stone wall. It was comprised of interlocking gray stones, each approximately about a foot in diameter. All of them appeared to be in their natural state, and, obviously, every stone was selected based on size to permit the construction of the wall without the benefit of mortar. The wall stood impressively before me. It was massive and tall. I wanted to see what was on the other side of this barrier, but I could not see anything except the immense block of stones.

Suddenly, beginning in the middle of the wall, the stones began to break out. I witnessed one stone after another fall away to the ground below me. As they did so, a gaping hole emerged in the structure. At first there appeared to be nothing on the other side.

I instinctively began to step through the wall, stretching out my right foot, lifting it up and over the group of fallen stones lying beneath me. As it came down on the other side, I was surprised to feel a hard surface under my foot. I looked down, noticing a narrow stone path immediately on the other side, which ended only a few feet in front of the wall. There was nothing else on the other side, except this small trail of stones, apparently leading nowhere. I finished stepping completely through the hole and began to advance to the end of the path.

As I did so, I was amazed to discover that with each step, the stone path expanded out farther and farther before me. An awesome picture began to materialize. One by one, tulips of every different color and shade vividly popped up as I ambled along. Each began with a single stem pushing through the earth, reaching full bloom within seconds. It was as if I was witnessing life emerging in time-lapse photography, instead of real time.

My stride got stronger and stronger with each step, as if the blossoming path and flowers were empowering me. The farther I traveled, the more the barren and blank ground transformed into a beautiful, colorful landscape. The flowers expanded out on either side of me exponentially. The sky, as well, changed from a nondescript gray tone to a deep blue hue.

Soon, I was standing on a path, extending out indefinitely among a sea of tulips, swaying in tandem with a light, cool breeze. It was a bright, sunny, spring day, invoking a sense of love of life and joy.

Charles asked me what I saw, which dissolved the scene in an instant. As I relayed the vision, he smiled. It was extraordinary, but I sensed he had come along with me on my journey, as he appeared to recognize the flowers were tulips even though I had not divulged the type of flowers in the landscape. Then he said something very profound. He told me that I could choose to bring forward a beautiful life, just like what I witnessed as I walked along the path. It was all up to me.

The vision provided a glimpse into a possible future. I could break down the walls in front of me, advancing to create my own world, thereby experiencing true joy for the first time in my life. It was a vision totally created by me, as Charles did not utter a word during the journey or provide any comments until afterwards.

Each of us has the ability to create our own path. It is my wish for others that they choose to allow the same for themselves. In the meantime, the journey continues . . .

About the Author

Cindy L. Herb has had an extensive career in the corporate environment, supported by a Bachelor of Fine Arts degree from Southern Methodist University. After meeting a shaman in 2007, Cindy began writing a cathartic journal of traumatic life experiences, especially those events centered on a childhood rape, which occurred while working as a newspaper carrier for a major cosmopolitan newspaper in Dallas. What evolved from this journey to healing was the book *Awakening the Spirit: The Open Wide Like a Floozy Chronicles*. Cindy has plans for a lecture series and additional books in the near future.